ME AND MY BIG MOUTH

Me and My Big Mouth

Larry Adler

with Philip Judge

Edited by William Hall

BLAKE

Published by Blake Publishing Ltd,
98–100 Great North Road, London N2 0NL, England

First published in Great Britain in 1994

ISBN 1 85782 087 8

British Library Cataloguing-in-Publication Data: A catalogue
record for this book is available from the British Library.

Typeset by DTP, Hemel Hempstead

Printed by Cox and Wyman, Reading, Berkshire

1 3 5 7 9 10 8 6 4 2

Without Elton John, George Martin, Jonathan Shalit and Sting it would have been impossible.

Dedicated to my children – Carole, Marmoset, Peter, Wendy; my brother and his wife – Jerry and Jean Adler; and my grandchildren – Emma and Susannah.

Contents

My thanks to:

Gloria Leighton, Trudie Styler, David and Tatiana Wilson.

Without the following my 80th birthday CD and book might not have happened: Roger Aimes, Annette Battam, Alan Benson, Howard Berman, David Blake, John Blake, Rick Blasky, David Clipsham, Chris Cook, William Hall, David Perez, Roger Watson and Issy van Randwyck.

Oleta Adams, Chris de Burgh, Kate Bush, Cher, Sinead O'Connor, Elvis Costello, Peter Gabriel, Elton John, Jon Bon Jovi, Meat Loaf, Robert Palmer, Courtney Pine, Carly Simon, Lisa Stansfield, Sting and Willard White.

Mark Knopfler and Richie Sambora.

In the studio: Giles Martin, Graham Preskett, Rupert Coulson, Geoff Foster, Cliff Jones and Steve Orchard. At Air Studios: Shirley Burns, John Burgess and Alison Burton.

Jonathan Shalit wishes to thank Leslie Aday, Darrin Barter, Ken Berry, Cody Burridge, Addie Churchill, Sylvia Coleman, Bernadette Coyle, Guy Cross, Samantha Clay, Paul Conroy, Harriet Constantine, Jacqui Derbyshire, Christine Dunmore, Kate Elworthy, Rob Fleming, Michael Gibb, Mark Goldberg, Theresa Green, Andrew Gummer, David Harper, Bas Hartong, Rick Holmes, Adrian Houston, Marsha Hunt, Michael Kamen, Robert Key, Paul Korzilius, Linda Lyon, Tommy Manzi, Steve Matthews, Julia Maynard, Sadie Mayne, Kaz Mercer, Claire Milner, Bruno Morelli, Nicky Neave, Martin Nelson, Annie Parsons, Deborah Porter, John Reid, Rosie Ries, Jake Riviera, Arlyne Rotherg, Caroline Ryan, Janine Schmidt, Billy Sammeth, Niki Sanderson, Bob Skoro, Carol Stockdale, Mike Storey, Sian Thomas, Tim Tuer, Nicola Turnbull, Caroline Underwood, Hilary Walker, Jo Weinberg, Annie Woolf.

IMP – Exclusively the best for Gershwin sheet music – 081 551 6131.

For further information on Larry Adler contact:
Sigmund Shalit & Associates
Cambridge Theatre
Seven Dials
Covent Garden
London WC2H 9HU
Tel: 44 (0) 71 379 3282
Fax: 44 (0) 71 379 3238.

Our gratitude and thanks to you all.

Foreword

Having written one volume of autobiography (a journalist asked me, 'Who's it about?') why do another? The first one was finished in 1983, and was published in 1984. A lot has happened since then.

In March of 1993 I had an invitation from Sting to play a song of his called 'The Shape of My Heart'. I was doubtful, mainly because I didn't think my style could fit his kind of music. (I hadn't yet heard any.) He sent me a cassette of the song that I liked a lot. I went to his recording studio and played the required ten bars. Then Sting suggested we do it again, and I just play wherever I felt like playing. The song was included on his Grammy-award-winning CD, *Ten Summoner's Tales*. Sting later invited me to join him for three concerts at the Royal Albert Hall. I asked him not to introduce me; his young fans wouldn't know who in hell I was. To my real surprise his fans did know me: they began to applaud as I came on.

Later, after the concert, I had a call from Sting. He had heard I was making a CD to celebrate my

coming eightieth birthday. Would I like him to
join me on it? I refused indignantly (and if you
believe that . . .).

I then wrote to Elton John. He phoned me from
Paris, delighted with my letter, and said, 'If you
really want me on the recording, count me in.'

Polygram was interested, and with the efforts of
impresario Jonathan Shalit, a collection of names
was built up. Oleta Adams, Larry Adler, Chris de
Burgh, Kate Bush, Cher, Sinead O'Connor, Elvis
Costello, Peter Gabriel, Elton John, Jon Bon Jovi,
George Martin, Meat Loaf, Robert Palmer, Courtney
Pine, Issy van Randwyck, Carly Simon, Lisa
Stansfield, Sting and Willard White. My own solo
would be the 'Rhapsody in Blue' and the musical
theme that linked each artist would be the songs of
George and Ira Gershwin. The unifying force that
held everything together was one of the finest gentle-
men I have ever known in the music world, George
Martin, the producer of the Beatles.

My first book was called, *It Ain't Necessarily So*.
Several titles were considered for this book. 'Name
Drops Keep Falling on My Head' was one and anyone who knows me can see the reason for that title.
'Hand to Mouth' was another; it had been the
working title of my first book. A candid friend had
suggested 'Embraceable Me', and someone had
called in on a radio show to suggest 'I Blew It' which
was good but too defeatist. My brother Jerry had
proposed, 'The Man I Love: An Autobiography',
which is my favourite. My publishers thought of *Me
and My Big Mouth* and, as I write, that is the title.

It occurs to me that, if you're interested in reading my story, you should know something about me in advance. Although I was born into an Orthodox Jewish family, it didn't take me long to lose my religion completely. I have no belief in the metaphysical, the paranormal or in anything for which confirmed evidence cannot be established. I have worked out a few three-word maxims that I try to live by, and which I tried to teach to my children. Anyway, my true religion is Orthodox Cowardice.

1. Think for yourself.
2. Guilt is personal.
3. What's the evidence?

I'll leave it at that. I don't like preaching yet I've just done it.

In my previous book, I felt that I hadn't been objective and that perhaps an outsider could do better. I had many interviews with Philip Judge. That done, I felt it better to stay away from the result. Thus I haven't seen the finished product nor tried in any way to edit anything. What you will read is what Philip Judge put down. It occurs to me that this may well be the world's first unauthorized autobiography.

Larry Adler

Hampstead, London, 1994.

1

Sting, Elton, Gershwin and Co.

'W.C. Fields warned us about working with children and animals. He forgot to mention Larry Adler.'

Sting

Wednesday 1 December 1993 dawned dull and overcast, with a hint of drizzle in the air. But nothing could dampen my spirits as I locked the door of my flat in Chalk Farm, north London, and climbed into the chauffeur-driven car that would take me up Haverstock Hill to the heights of Hampstead and the converted church on the corner of Lyndhurst Road that was now the studios of Air, otherwise George Martin's Associated Independent Recording company.

The huge red-brick Victorian grade-two listed building towers like a monolith across the road from the Royal Free Hospital. From the outside, it still looks like a church, with its stained-glass windows and Gothic rooftop.

Inside, you feel you've stepped into the film *2001*.

George wrote his own name into musical history when he became producer of the Beatles, and indeed became known as 'the fifth Beatle'. But today the twelve-foot wide bank of coloured buttons that control forty-eight tracks behind the dark glass of the control room are part of a whole new world. As someone once said, they make the fuzzy old pictures of George fiddling with big brown knobs on a console in Abbey Road look like something out of 'Thunderbirds'.

Tall, quietly-spoken, with a mass of grey hair flopping around his ears, George could be anyone's favourite uncle. He happens to be one of the most respected figures in the business, a man who has watched the world's legendary names pass through the arched portals and electronic gates into his private empire. Not to worship, but to create a different kind of music amid the extraordinary acoustics of the former Congregational church.

The acoustics were judged superb under public scrutiny when, in December 1992, Prince Charles attended a triumphant gala performance of *Under Milk Wood* scored by George. Top groups like Dire Straits use it as their second home.

But even by George's standards, today is rather special. I am there to record my tribute to one of the world's great composers – a CD called *The Glory of Gershwin* that will not only mark my eightieth birthday, but bring together under one roof some of the biggest names in the music business: Elton John, Sting, Chris de Burgh and many more.

The thrill for me is that aided and abetted by my trusty mouth organ, I'm backing them in every number.

George looms up at the door, shakes my hand in greeting. 'Come on in, Larry. We're ready for you.'

George is an interesting man, although I suppose this is rather like saying the *Queen Mary* was a nice little boat, or that Concorde has a fairly good turn of speed.

In fact, this legend in the music field fell into record producing by accident. He was an oboist, trained by Margaret Asher (mother of actress Jane), and his ambition was to be an aircraft designer. At the age of twenty-two he took on the modest job of an assistant at EMI on their Parlophone label.

In next to no time – give or take a few years – he was head of Parlophone, recording albums by such diverse talents as Peter Sellers and the Goons, Shirley Bassey, Matt Munro and Stan Getz, not to mention the classical batons waved in his direction by the likes of Sir Malcolm Sargent and Sir Adrian Boult.

Then came the Beatles, and George Martin's life, times and career turned a somersault into mega-success. The rest – and for once the cliché is true – is musical history.

I had first met him four months previously, and instantly we became old friends. I would like to put on record that in my book – this one, now I think of it – George is a true gentleman. Even if, at sixty-eight, he's a mere stripling compared to me.

Inside his personal palace, the surroundings are

almost surrealistic. Panelled walls, big curved windows of stained glass, an upstairs gallery for the overflow of the old congregation. And along one wall, massive organ pipes towering up to the blue domed ceiling like a salvo of leaden grey shells waiting to be launched. The hexagonal floor can accommodate up to six hundred people under the vast roof.

The sounds of a sixty-piece orchestra tuning up fill the air. In the far corner a familiar figure sits at a black concert grand piano picking out the notes of 'Someone to Watch Over Me': Elton John, in a loud black-and-white check sports jacket and black shirt. He spots me, waves a lazy hand in greeting, and bends back to the keyboard, the studio lights gleaming on his gold-rimmed spectacles as he toys with the notes that he will sing later.

Chris de Burgh appears. 'Hi, Larry. Good to meet you at last.' A sturdy, compact man with an effervescent grin, he has just flown in from Dublin and rushed straight from the airport to make it. The soulful singer of 'Lady in Red' will be adding his weight with 'Do What You Do!' to this unique album.

I hadn't met him before. I thought I'd better find something out. 'Can you play the mouth organ, just in case I keel over and die in the middle of it?' I inquire, deadpan.

'I wouldn't dare!' Chris rejoins. 'Only you can do it.' Nice of him to say that, and I nod appreciatively.

'True,' I tell him.

At any major recording session there is always a

lot of joking and leg-pulling to ease the tension. You can feel it crackling like electricity in the air the moment you walk in to any studio, and I've been in enough of them to know what's coming. You do your best to control the butterflies, but even the biggest star knows how much depends on him, and feels the adrenalin pumping.

The musicians themselves are brisk and businesslike. They, too, know the score, in every sense. And they sense the excitement in the air.

Inside the recording booth, its bewildering control system like the flightdeck of Concorde, another figure detaches himself from a corner where he has been studying the two numbers he will perform. Sting is dressed in a casual brown woollen waistcoat over a white cricketing sweater. His face under the close-cropped sandy hair lights up and he shakes my hand vigorously. 'Great to see you again.'

We had not met since the previous year, when I joined him in three concerts at the Albert Hall. Now, as we go through the score of 'Nice Work If You Can Get It', we find we have something more in common than music: mouth organs, believe it or not. 'I learned to play at school,' Sting recalls. 'But only the diatonic kind.'

That's the easy one, without sharps or flats. Me, I play the chromatic mouth organ, with the little button on the side that you press to raise the music half a tone. Sting is generous enough to add: 'You, my friend, are out of my league.' Well, I hope so, I tell him!

Sting and Elton and I chat about music and the good times.

Elton nearly didn't make our session – and I wouldn't have blamed him. We had first met at a show-business dinner at Claridge's. He came up to my table in his peaked cap with his hand outstretched – singing the theme from *Genevieve* which I had composed back in 1953 and which had been nominated for an Oscar. And he sang it loud!

Luckily he only knew the tune: the words are terrible! Can you imagine Elton singing: 'Genevieve, Genevieve, light as a feather you walked from heaven right into my heart . . .'? It's not even about a car.

But then he held out his hand to my companion, a lovely raven-haired Peruvian lady named Tatiana who was my lover for eight years and who runs the Cafe Delancey in Camden Town.

To my astonishment and dismay Tatiana became all prim and proper. 'I don't shake hands with people who keep their hat on in my presence,' she said stiffly.

Elton just looked at her, dropped his hand, and walked off.

I turned on her, knowing the high stakes ahead. 'For Christ's sake, you could have blown the whole thing!'

Tatiana gave me one of her 'so what?' looks, and that was that. She is some lady, and always manages to surprise me when I least expect it – which, I guess, is the point of a surprise.

Luckily Elton hadn't taken umbrage. I dropped

him a letter, telling him about the tribute to Gershwin, asking if he was interested. He called me from Paris. 'If you want me, I'm your man.' Wonderful!

In the studio, his interpretation of 'Someone to Watch Over Me' is heart-rending. He stands by the big concert grand, I'm on a stool at his knee with my own microphone. We work on it for more than two hours till we get it right, and if I tell you that the final version brings tears to my eyes – and I know that tune forwards, backwards and sideways – you will realize just how special is the result of our joint labours.

Most people have no idea just how hard musicians work to get the sound they want when they cut a disc. That first day turned into a long one: it was midnight before I was finally able to leave the converted church and drive home. All in all, we had been at it for fourteen hours. Four down, a mere fourteen to go!

That day set the tone for the other celebrity singers who would follow. The list reads like a roll call of modern musical mega-stars touching finger-tips with the magic of an immortal: Oleta Adams singing 'Embraceable You', Kate Bush with 'The Man I Love', Cher with 'It Ain't Necessarily So', Elvis Costello with 'But not for Me', Peter Gabriel and Courtney Pine with – one of my own personal favourites – 'Summertime', Jon Bon Jovi with 'How Long Has This Been Going On?', Sinead O'Connor with 'My Man's Gone Now', Meat Loaf with 'Some-body Loves Me', Robert Palmer with 'I Got Rhythm', Carly Simon with 'I've Got a Crush on You', Lisa Stansfield with 'They Can't Take That Away from Me', and Willard White with 'Bidin' My Time'.

Pause for breath. Oh, I'm almost forgetting one other: a beautiful young lady named Issy van Randwyck, a comparative newcomer with a voice like a dream. She belts out 'I'll Build a Stairway to Paradise'.

Issy and I once appeared on the BBC's lunchtime TV show 'Pebble Mill' broadcast from their Birmingham studios. She sang 'Summertime' while I accompanied her on mouth organ and piano – and what a lovely sound it was. We returned in triumph to London, where my old friend and tennis rival Victor Lownes told me he had kindly recorded it on video for me.

When he sent it over to my flat, I found it was in double time. My interview was a gabble, the piano and harmonica raced through the prelude, and as for Issy – oh dear! It will never sell.

When I called Victor he pleaded that his machine must have gong wrong. Hmmm! Knowing Victor's sense of humour, I still have my doubts.

In fact Issy is a Dutch baroness, who had her own cabaret show at London's Pizza on the Park. Through her I met an exciting young impresario named Jonathan Shalit, who seemed overwhelmed by the rapport I had with young people – whether playing at the Edinburgh Festival, or the Albert Hall.

Jonathan turned out to be a Gershwin fan. I took him to a Sting concert, and an idea was formed. He approached the Polygram label and suggested Sting and Elton to head a host of star names to make *The Glory of Gershwin*. They went for it – and Jonathan went for George Martin, the only producer in the world he felt could do justice to such an immense project. George didn't need that much persuading . . . and the names rolled in.

The only question was whether we should sell out to pure commercialism, or record in the traditional way I knew Gershwin would have liked. No second guess needed – that's the way we did it – traditional.

Why Gershwin? I have met many composers, from Cole Porter to Richard Rodgers, from Ravel to Rachmaninov, and respected them all. But the one I admired most has to be George Gershwin, the master of experimental jazz, born Jacob Gershvin in 1898. He could touch the hearts of people everywhere, and that's why I chose him for the album.

He is also the only composer to have made the great cross-over from jazz into the classical field.

Our first meeting was not auspicious. At the age of sixteen, I was a sparky kid trying anything to get my foot another rung up the ladder. You've heard the expression 'rich and running'? Well, I wasn't rich, but I was running – here, there, anywhere. Plaguing agents for work. Sneaking backstage to see if someone would offer me a job. My effrontery amazes me even now.

One night I was standing outside the stage door of the Roxy Theater in New York, playing my mouth organ at anyone who came out, hoping to hear the magic words: 'Hey, I *like* that!' Bandleader Paul Whiteman and his orchestra were playing inside, backing his film *King of Jazz*, which was an early talkie in glorious Technicolor. It featured great numbers like 'Happy Feet', 'Ragamuffin Romeo', and 'It Happened in Monterey', along with a fresh-faced young singer named Bing Crosby and the Rhythm Boys.

The jazz sax player Frankie Trumbauer was heading past me for the stage door, when he pulled up short. He listened for a few minutes, then beckoned me with a finger. I followed him through, and along a passage to a dressing-room door. Inside, Whiteman was chatting to another man.

'Paul,' said Trumbauer. 'Listen to this kid.'

Without further ado I launched into 'When Day is Done', cheating a little because I cribbed it from Whiteman's own interpretation.

The bandleader frowned, nodded, then said: 'Let me hear you play "Rhapsody in Blue".'

Now this piece of Gershwin brilliance was far too complex for me to handle, though later it would become a favourite in my repertoire. In those days, however, no chance. But I wasn't going to admit it.

Loftily I said: 'Sorry, I don't like "Rhapsody in Blue".'

Whiteman turned to the young man sitting across from him. 'What do you think of that, George? This kid doesn't *like* "Rhapsody in Blue"!'

That's how I met Gershwin.

It was at the house of his elder brother Ira that George astounded me one day by giving me his own verdict on the best of the best. It was one of those informal gatherings on a sunny weekend in Hollywood, and we were standing around the patio chatting and drinking. Inside, Ira's educated fingers flickered over the keys of his concert grand.

George gestured around at the throng. They included Richard Rodgers, Johnny Green, Irving Berlin, Cole Porter and Harold Arlen – who wrote those all-timers 'Stormy Weather', 'That Ol' Black Magic' and 'One for My Baby'. George pointed at Arlen. 'You know what, Larry? He's the best of all of us.'

I couldn't believe it. 'What are you saying, George? *Why?*'

'Because he takes risks,' Gershwin said in his direct way. 'A lot of composers get themselves tied up in a complicated harmonic situation, and take the easy way out. Arlen never does.'

I didn't agree, and told him so. I still don't. Any of those men in that house would have given anything to have been able to write *Porgy and Bess*.

Ira, of course, wrote the lyrics to that 1935 master-piece of black American opera. But it was not until 1983 that he finally revealed his own favourite – and that was when he was on his deathbed. I visited him two months before he died. As I sat by the bed he suddenly reached out and grabbed my wrist.

'You want to hear my favourite lyric?' he rasped. 'Listen to this:

"Penicillin, streptomycin,
Make a highball – put some ice in!"'

That was Ira. Warm, caring, funny, and game to the last.

George was never a bar-fly. He didn't hang out like so many musicians do. We would always meet at Ira's place, and if we weren't sitting around chatting or having a musical session I would challenge him to a game of tennis on Ira's court behind the house.

The problem there was that George was a terrible loser. So to keep him happy I always let him win – and he was only too happy to give me a game!

George forgave me for that first outrageous gaffe, though it was five years and countless stage and variety shows later before I had a chance to make amends.

I was due to sail to Southampton on the *Aquitania* with C.B. Cochran to try my luck in Britain. He had offered me no contract, I paid my own expenses, I got no guarantees. But Charles Cochran – known as 'Cockie' to his intimates, and ever the persuasive showman – had assured me that a new chapter of my life would unfold.

The night before I sailed, a certain Jules Glaenzer gave a farewell party for me at his house in the affluent East 60s side of New York. Glaenzer – make that Mr Glaenzer – was the millionaire vice-president of Cartier's and threw the best theatrical parties in town. His magnificent mansion boasted two concert Steinways, and if you were fortunate enough to get an invite, you didn't turn it down.

On a number of occasions I met Howard Hughes at a Glaenzer party. He would tower over me in his dinner jacket and scuffed shoes, and smile benignly down at me while I chattered away, nodding every now and then – in total silence. He never spoke a single word to me except to acknowledge my greeting. I still wonder if he ever heard anything I said.

By now I was making something of a name for myself, could count on bringing in $350 a week, minimum, and was on most of the party lists. Even so I was touched and flattered by the quality of the guests Mr Glaenzer had assembled for my going-away party. All the men were in white tie and tails – except me. Somehow I had never got round to investing in a tail suit, though it would be the first thing I did when I got to London. No matter. The guest of honour was allowed his little quirk.

I provided most of the entertainment, playing 'Body and Soul' with Johnny Green, 'Blue Skies' with Irving Berlin, 'Mountain Greenery' with Richard Rodgers and 'But in the Morning, No' with Cole Porter.

Around midnight Mr Glaenzer called for silence. He was actually known – behind his back – as the Great Shusher. 'Listen, everyone. Larry and George are going to play the "Rhapsody in Blue" . . .' The room burst into spontaneous applause.

I was? We were? Our host hadn't asked us, or even hinted at it. I had never attempted the number, though I knew the Paul Whiteman record-

ing. I caught the bandleader's eye across the room.
I knew what he was thinking. George, too, looked
pretty dubious. He didn't know whether I could
handle it, and neither did I. But it was too late to
back down.

George sat himself down at the Steinway, I stood
by his side, and began with the notes usually taken
by the clarinet. George came in at the top of the run
– and we were off and away.

I'll never forget that magical moment. It was one
of those times when two musicians are in total
rapport, working by instinct, the one taking over as
the other fell away. I had the tune in my head,
which is the way I always work – no song sheets.
I knew when to lay out and let the piano take over.
George would signal me back in at the right
moment. The doubt in his face melted away, and
was replaced by the intense joy you knew he always
felt when he played. Or maybe, this time, it was
relief.

We finished together on that five-chord piano
climax, while I held the high F. The room erupted
into cheering. Ethel Merman enveloped me in a
bear-hug, the kind that makes your eyes water.
Vivienne Segal, the reigning Broadway musical star
of *Pal Joey* and *Desert Song*, kissed me.

I came out from under to find George Gershwin
gripping my hand. He fixed me with an odd look.
'The goddamn thing sounds as if I wrote it for you,'
he said. And his face broke into a smile.

The goddamn thing still does. I can't count the
times I have played it, with just a piano or with a

full orchestra, but it always gives me goose-bumps.

The only downside was that whenever I broached the idea of George writing something for the mouth organ, he would tell me: 'I already have!'

George Gershwin died on 11 July 1937, succumbing in a Hollywood hospital during an operation for a benign brain tumour. He was an East Side boy who played ragtime by day and studied Dvořák and Debussy by night. As the broadcaster and jazz authority Alistair Cooke summed up in his tribute: 'Of all the gifted men who made the twenties and thirties a golden age of song, Gershwin was the truest original.'

I had an intriguing insight into George's condition. At one point in my life I was under analysis for a brief time. My psychiatrist Ernst Simmel also had George Gershwin on his books. After the composer's death, Dr Simmel revealed to me how, when Gershwin first came to him, he was complaining of migraine headaches which he thought might be neurotic.

Simmel always asked new patients to have a complete medical check-up. In George's case, he recommended a spinal tap. George dreaded the pain of it, and refused to have one.

The analyst told me that had Gershwin undergone the spinal tap it is possible that the fluid would have shown evidence of the brain tumour that eventually killed him.

But the composer had other warnings. I was in the audience when he appeared with the Los Angeles Philharmonic at a concert in LA. In the third movement of the Concerto in F, something strange happened: George stopped playing for a few bars, stared fixedly out at the audience, then resumed playing.

Weird. Afterwards Ira Gershwin hosted a party for the musicians and invited guests.

I went up to George. 'What happened?' I asked, without preamble.

'Well,' George said, frowning. 'During the third movement I could swear I smelled burning rubber. I thought that maybe the place was on fire. I stopped, looked around, saw nothing, no panic – so I went on playing.'

What none of us realized at the time, and couldn't know, was that if someone smells burning rubber – and there isn't any – it is a possible clue to a brain tumour.

Weeks later George collapsed outside his brother's home, and sat on the kerb holding his head in his hands. People ran up to help, and he was rushed to hospital.

But it was too late. My friend died at the age of thirty-nine. All I could think was: what a tragic, useless waste. John O'Hara wrote: 'George Gershwin is dead, but I don't have to believe it if I don't want to.'

Shortly after his death, his brother Ira showed up unexpectedly on the doorstep of the house where I was living in Beverly Hills. He was carrying a large box.

He said: 'Larry, I think your neck size is about the same as George's. I know he'd like you to have these.' Inside were dress shirts, white waistcoats, white ties – I wore them for many years afterwards at concerts and shows.

So – why Gershwin on the album? For our moments together. For the fun and the laughter. For the riches to be found in his music by prospectors like me and those similarly inclined. There was no one like George.

That's why.

2

Early Days

*'I've never seen anyone play the harmonica
like Larry. I thought he was going to
swallow it.'*

Elton John

In 1914 a number of events of historical significance occurred. Marconi transmitted wireless telephone messages between two Italian ships fifty miles apart. The Panama Canal was completed. Picasso painted his cubist 'The Small Table'. Edgar Rice Burroughs wrote the first Tarzan book, *Tarzan of the Apes*.

Oh yes, and on 28 June some nut called Gavrilo Princip assassinated Archduke Franz Ferdinand on the streets of Sarajevo and sparked off the First World War.

Apart from all that, I was born on 10 February, which to me was an event of far greater significance than anything else. The place: Baltimore, a town from which I spent the first fourteen years of my life plotting my escape.

Nobody seemed to like anybody. Catholics,

Protestants, Poles, Blacks, Jews – all cordially detested or merely feared one another. Much as it is today, I imagine, only more widespread.

My full name was, and still is, Lawrence Cecil Adler. My young brother, born five years later, was called Hilliard Gerald. Where Mother got those names from I have no idea, but as you'll gather she did us no favours.

Lawrence was considered a sissy name by all the Chucks, Buzzes, Stus and Chips who surrounded me in the classroom at Junior High. And as for Cecil – oh, wow! I kept that one quiet.

I was the smallest kid on the block, short-sighted, wore glasses, and was inevitably nicknamed Four Eyes. I started learning jokes at an early age to make the bigger boys laugh. Not to be popular, because I've never worried about my popularity, but to avoid being beaten up. Humour is a great defence mechanism for turning away wrath.

In fact, I survived the rigours of the playground thanks to a big kid named Reese Whittemore. In the first week of term, another boy tried to take my marbles away from me. In the middle of our yelling match this heavy-set, muscular lad with a crewcut came up. He grabbed my marbles from the other kid, handed them back to me, and announced darkly: 'Anyone troubles you, I'll beat the crap outa them!'

From that moment I was left alone. Better still, I was allowed into Reese's gang, a signal honour which made me virtually inviolate throughout the rest of my time at school. He became my hero, so it

was something of a let-down when I reached nineteen and read that Reese Whittemore had been sent
to the electric chair in Maryland for a murder committed during a bank robbery. Had I stayed with his
gang, I might have been in on that job and seen the
inside of Death Row myself.

Instead, at fourteen, I went on the stage.

There were no early signs to show it might
happen. My father Louis was a plumber with his
own truck, which had the sign ADLER'S PLUMBING
SHOP ON WHEELS proudly emblazoned along the side
in black letters. My dad took pride in his work, no
doubt of that, and would let me join him on some
of the jobs when he was called out. But watching
him dig a ditch and laboriously place a drainpipe in
it convinced me that wherever my future lay, it did
not include a career in plumbing.

We lived at No. 774, Columbia Avenue, later
renamed Washington Boulevard. The area was
modest, to put it politely. Trolley-cars ran past the
house, and their rumbling shook the walls.

Mother was a beautiful woman named Sadie,
with long black hair that reached to the ground. My
first memory is being held in her arms as she sat in
the side-car of Dad's motorbike being driven through
the streets of Baltimore – I must have been two.

Another early memory is of my hating the sound
of a whistle. I have always been sensitive to sound,
can't stand eating noises – which are bad manners,
anyway – and I've been known to get up and leave
a table rather than listen to someone slurping their
soup.

But whistling is still the sound I find most irritating, and I will cross the street rather than walk anywhere near someone whistling. I don't know why – but there is *one* possible explanation. Dad used to summon me into the house by blowing on a family whistle: three short blasts with a rising inflection on the third. All I needed was a collar and a bone, and I could have changed my name to Fido. Perhaps my phobia is Freudian, after all.

Where did my musical ability stem from? Step forward, Aunt Annie! Her full name was Annie Serotkin, she was my mother's sister, and she was a glorious lady who lived into her nineties. Her house was nearby, and I would spend long and happy hours with her, sitting on her knee while she taught little Larry songs. Rude songs.

Yes, Aunt Annie was a character straight out of James Joyce – ribald, profane, with a sense of humour that was unashamedly vulgar, as I found out when I grew older and realized what the words meant. In fact, she taught me to sing before I learned to talk.

She also taught me my first jokes, the ones that would prove so invaluable in the playground, and lead to others that would help get me through life.

We had a piano in the house, a Kimball upright which Mother had won by supplying the last line in a limerick competition. So humour must run in the family. I just wish I knew what that last line had been.

When I started the first hesitant steps in learning the piano, I found I could pick out tunes by ear, and even harmonize them. Two years of piano lessons did me little good. Scales bored me, and I always held my hands low, actually below the keyboard, so that only my fingers came over the top like spider's legs.

Years later Artur Rubinstein, the Polish-born prodigy who was playing Chopin in public at the age of eleven, stared at my hands as I played and proclaimed loudly: *'Impossible!'* Well, I did it.

The piano and I fell out of love with each other when I was sent to study at the Peabody Conservatory of Music at Mount Vernon Place in Baltimore. I was never a good pupil anyway. For the student recital, which was obligatory after two terms, I prepared a Grieg waltz based on my imitation of Rachmaninov's recording. I was nearly twelve, and thought my interpretation was even better than the Master's.

The supervisor was a middle-aged woman with a bust like the prow of an aircraft-carrier and an expression to match. She eyed me sternly through her pince-nez as I sat down at the piano, and said: 'And what are we going to play, my little man?'

I know I was pint-sized, but goddammit, *we* weren't going to play anything. *I* was, and I didn't like being patronized. To hell with the Grieg waltz, I thought, showing early signs of the cussedness that would become such a lovable part of my nature in later life. I charged into a rip-roaring version of 'Yes, We Have no Bananas', glaring defiance at tits-and-pince-nez while the music room echoed to the cheers of the other pupils.

She stopped me after twelve bars. 'Thank you. That will do. We have heard *quite* enough!' She sent me home, and followed it up next morning with a letter to my parents telling them to keep me there. I was expelled. At the time I regarded it as a unique distinction, and still do.

Perhaps I should mention that I was nine years old when I won a spelling contest with the word 'sanguineous'. It simply means 'bloody'. I like to think I have been sanguineous-minded ever since.

I first touched a mouth organ when I was nine. My parents gave it to me as a birthday present, and in a few weeks I could play half a dozen tunes on it. Learning to play the mouth organ isn't hard. Learning to play it *well* – now *that's* hard!

The one they gave me was the chromatic mouth organ. That's the one, as Sting and I would discuss years later when we were comparing notes, with a button on the side that you press to raise the music that vital half-tone that creates a new horizon of sound. If it hadn't been chromatic, I would probably never have learned to play – because I wanted to get all the notes.

The other kind, the diatonic with no sharps or flats that performers like Bob Dylan play, just doesn't interest me. The chromatic mouth organ gives you a chance to develop your own style – Stevie Wonder, for instance, gets an incredible sound that I can't get. It's his sound. Just as I've got *my* sound. Another with his own style is the Belgian virtuoso Toots Thielemans.

I can teach you to play in two lessons, after which you'll be able to produce a simple song. The keyboard is easy to master. The hardest thing is simply to get a musical sound. But I can't teach anyone to get *my* sound, any more than a top concert violinist like Jascha Heifetz could teach a pupil to get *his* sound. It can't be done. You've got to be an original.

Oddly enough, the mouth organ I had as a kid of nine is virtually the same size as the one I use today. It had ten holes, embracing just one complete octave. Today I use twelve holes, with a three-octave range.

If you're my pupil, the first thing I teach you is to play a scale. I write out where the notes are on a sheet of foolscap, show you where the holes are, and that's how you learn to play a simple scale. Once you can do that, I'll write out an easy song for you.

OK, I know that everybody calls it a harmonica. Or they did. And I know it's still in the dictionaries: 'HARMONICA: A small, rectangular musical instrument consisting of a row of free reeds set back in air holes, played by exhaling or inhaling.'

Remember that immortal line delivered by Lauren Bacall to Humphrey Bogart: 'Just whistle. You know how to whistle, don't you? All you have to do is put your lips together – and blow!' Well, I blow – and suck.

Personally, I always felt 'harmonica' was too prissy and genteel a term for it, like holding up your little finger when you have a cup of tea.

In addition, I was aware that the Germans call an accordion the *Hundharmonica*, and that Mozart wrote a work for the *Glassharmonica*: glasses filled with water played by running fingers round their rims. I felt 'mouth organ' was more of a generic term, closer to the real thing, and so I've called it that ever since.

In any case, I always preferred a short word to a long one.

What really turns me on to the mouth organ is the *humanity* of it, the fact that you can express something so near to the human voice. First, you're so close to the instrument that you look as if you're in danger of swallowing it. If you play it really well you can express yourself completely, finding an emotional sound that you cannot get on any other instrument in the world. All right, I'm biased. But it's true.

When I'm at my best, I can produce a sound that is quite eerie, a kind of singing, almost human. You don't get that effect every time, believe me. It comes by chance, not by inspiration. It can happen that day – or it can't. But after it does I walk on air for the rest of the day.

It is this quality that reduced Pete Murray to genuine tears when I appeared on his LBC talk show in London in the winter of 1993. He put on my record of *Carmen* – and after it was over he could hardly speak. He was man enough to admit on the air: 'I'm in tears!' Now *that's* something that doesn't happen too often. A few minutes later a woman rang in from her car phone to tell us she had been forced to stop in a lay-by because she was in floods of tears too.

That's when you know you've reached them.

People ask me how many songs I've got in my repertoire. The answer is: I can play anything! How's that for modesty? But it's true – from violin concertos to jazz, I learn simply by putting a record on and picking it up by ear.

That's how I learned Vivaldi, Bach, you name it. I appeared with Isaac Stern for Bach's double violin concerto, playing one of the violin parts with my mouth organ – all learned by ear. I don't need a musical score in front of me. Anything I can get into my head, I can play.

The fact is that if I had stayed with the piano I could never have been in the same league as Rachmaninov or Vladimir Horowitz. But with the mouth organ ... Nobody existed before me. I was the world's first soloist.

I'm a footnote in musical history, but it's nice to know you've achieved that. And even nicer to know that for over half a century you have been considered the best at what you do.

Starting out, I learned show business the hard way. I was stage-struck, movie-struck, and had the best of both worlds when I could slip into Loew's Theater in Baltimore to catch a film, plus a stage show. At the Metropolitan, at the age of thirteen, I saw *The Jazz Singer* four times, largely because eight years previously, aged five, I had been taken to see

Al Jolson, live, in *Sinbad*, and even at that tender age realized he was a pretty special fellow. In fact I would say I became his number one fan.

A cousin of his named Harry Jolson owned a tailor's shop near us, and Dad persuaded him to make me a costume like Al's. I wore it to a Hallowe'en party, blacked up like Jolson, and happily pranced around the streets shouting: 'Trick or treat!' to startled passers-by.

Fifteen years later, when I had made it to Hollywood and was actually on the bill at the famed Grauman's Chinese Theater, I was having lunch at the Brown Derby with my agent Bill Perlberg – yes, I'd got myself an agent by then, and with the equally famed William Morris outfit – when a man came up, and stood over us. He said 'Hi' to Bill, then looked at me. 'I saw your act last night,' he said. 'The music's way too loud, kid. I told Grauman to take it down. Better for you.' And he turned and walked back to his table.

I stared after him. 'Who was that busybody?' I demanded.

Bill shook his head in disbelief. 'Didn't you recognize him? That was Al Jolson.'

I could have slid under the table. The one star in the whole showbiz firmament I rated above all others, and I hadn't uttered a word to him.

They say lightning never strikes twice. Whoever 'they' are, they're wrong. Move on another five years, and I'm at the Coconut Grove in Hollywood. Just as I'm about to play my last number, someone calls out from the tables: 'Play "Sonny Boy"!'

Now I don't like 'Sonny Boy'. And that night I am in a bad mood, I can't remember why. So I climb on to that famous invisible soapbox I keep in the wings, and deliver a pompous lecture on why I wouldn't be caught dead playing 'Sonny Boy'. Then I give them my final number, and walk off.

My partner Paul Draper, a tap-dancer, is waiting for me. He grabs my arm, and hisses: 'Larry, if I had a baseball bat, I'd beat the bejesus out of you. You know who called out for "Sonny Boy"?'

You've guessed it. 'Al Jolson, that's who.'

I stop dead in my tracks. Then without a word I turn and stride back out on stage. 'Ladies and gentlemen,' I tell them, 'I have just heard that the best reason for playing "Sonny Boy" is here in the room. I would be honoured to play it.'

And I play to my childhood hero.

I was a skinny kid around 5 foot 2 inches tall, and looked like Eddie Cantor. At the age of twelve I entered my first mouth organ contest – in agony. The event was to decide Baltimore's male and female champions. They would be pitted against each other to decide the Maryland State Championship. As the great day approached, I felt a growing ache in my gums – an abscessed tooth, would you believe. When I stepped out on to the rostrum, my jaw looked as if I'd got a tennis ball lodged in it.

I couldn't speak, but I could suck and I could blow. The other kids played popular tunes like

'Black Bottom' and 'St Louis Blues'. I gave them the
Minuet in G by Beethoven. Possibly because the
leading judge was Gustav Strube, founder and
conductor of the Baltimore Symphony Orchestras, I
won. He gave young Lawrence Cecil Adler 'ninety-
nine and nine-tenths' marks, then looked at me
and shrugged apologetically, adding: 'No von is
pairfect!'

Through the lump in my gum I mumbled my
thanks in muffled tones. The play-off against the
girls' section proved a walkover – and I found
myself State Champion, with a silver-plated cup to
take home in pride.

Personally, I think I deserved that award for
stoicism.

Two years later, I ran away from home. I had just
$35 in my pocket, saved over the months, but it was
enough to get me to New York on the four-hour
train ride from Union Station, and leave some
spending money over besides.

New York . . . Broadway . . . Manhattan . . . Fifth
Avenue . . . Times Square . . . It wasn't just the
glamorous names that lured me. A month before,
I had met Nat Brusiloff, the lead violinist with the
NBC Orchestra, at a friend's house near my
home in Baltimore. He heard me play, and was
impressed.

'You're OK, kid,' he said. 'If you ever come to
New York, look me up.'

Did he really think I wouldn't?

Nat let me stay in his house. He had a spare room
which was small but more than adequate. I'd have

slept in a shed if I had to. But first he made me call home, and reassure my parents I was all right.

As politely as possible I told Mother that if they forced me to come home, I'd only run away again. And this time I wouldn't call. 'This is where I want to be, Mother. Just let me have a chance to see if I can do it,' I pleaded.

Dad checked it out with Nat, and finally I got the nod. Whoopee! Then came the dampener. Where do I start?

Wandering through Manhattan, I spotted a poster for Borrah Minevich and his Harmonica Rascals. Promising. I told Nat about it, he pulled a few strings – and two days later I was presenting myself at the Manhattan Theater for an audition.

In Minevich's dressing-room, the great man sat in a chair and fixed me with a scowl which did not waver as I played him the Minuet in G that had made me State Champion. I got the impression he was there under some form of duress. To make matters worse, the rest of the Rascals were lined up in the doorway and corridor listening.

I came to the end with a flourish, and bowed. Minevich gave me his considered verdict. 'Kid,' he said 'you *stink*!'

On my way back up 44th and Broadway, close to tears, I stared out of the streetcar window, and noticed a crowd around the marquee of the New York Paramount. I could hear the squeals of the young girls clustered around the stage door as a man fought his way through, wearing the fixed smile of a celebrity hating every moment of it but pretending he loves you all, folks. Rudy Vallee. He was the idol of his day. The man who held the torch that would later be picked up by the likes of Elvis Presley, Mick Jagger, Rod Stewart, any of the Osmonds, and on into the names you've got on my Gershwin album!

Oh yes, Rudy was big-time. He was the first pop singer ever to be labelled a crooner, and the first singer to know the joys (or otherwise) of inducing mass swooning among the young and old in his audience. Croon or swoon, Rudy's nickname was the Vagabond Lover, named after his most successful song. It was also chosen as the title for his movie debut in 1929.

His trademark was a cardboard megaphone, which stood in for the microphone that had yet to be invented. I would grow to like the man's humour: in the 1970s he tried to get the street on which he lived in Los Angeles renamed 'Rue de Vallee'. The city council turned him down. They had no style. But like I say, the guy had a sense of humour.

It was notably lacking this day. The posters outside the Paramount announced: RUDY VALLEE AND HIS CONNECTICUT YANKEES. I thought quickly. Then rang the bell, jumped off the streetcar as it slowed down, and ran back to the theatre. The stage doorman had his hands full. The police had been called in by now to quell a near-riot, and sweating cops in blue with their peaked caps askew over one eye were struggling to keep the mob at bay.

I chose my moment. Plaintive squeals like those

of stuck pigs rose from the far side: 'Ru-dee! Rudee!'
Some young girl was having hysterics.

While everyone's attention was distracted, I
slipped through the cordon and past the doorman
and through the stage door, walking with as much
confidence as I could muster. First rule: walk, don't
run – just like they say at the traffic lights.

I was in, and searching for Rudy's dressing-room.
A flight of stairs faced me. I went up, searching each
floor. And up. No one tried to stop me. Rudy was
on the twelfth. His door was open, and he sat at the
mirror in front of a forest of naked lightbulbs
making up for the show.

His reflection stared at me as I hovered in the
doorway. 'What do you want, kid?'

I told him I played the mouth organ, and that I
wanted a job.

Rudy said: 'Look, kid, I'm just the master of
ceremonies.'

'Please,' I said. 'Just listen to me. Please – '

He looked at me. 'OK. Make it quick.'

I was sneaky. I played one of his hits: 'S'posin''.
When I had finished, he eyed me coldly. 'Save
your money, kid. You're a one-time novelty. Once
the people see you, that's it. You've got nothing else
to offer.'

'Well, thanks for your time,' I said. This was
turning into a great day. In the morning, I'm told I
stink. In the afternoon I'm told I'm a loser. Roll on,
nightfall.

Twenty years later I was guest on a New York
radio chat show, talking about my career, taking

questions from listeners. Out of the blue, in the last five minutes of air time, Rudy Vallee called in.

'I'm surprised you didn't mention me,' he said reprovingly. 'I gave you your first break, remember?'

Oh yeah?

But I had *chutzpah*, and that's what saved me.

Dictionary definition: 'Chutzpah: Slang: Shameless impudence, gall.' My definition, and I can't remember where I heard it: 'Chutzpah: A man who murders his mother and father, and asks for mercy from the court because he's an orphan.'

I wasn't going to give up that easily.

I was taken on by Paramount theatres on a forty-four-week contract at $100 a week to tour the States with various shows. In 1928, we're talking *money*.

I was under-age, and it was illegal for me to be working, but no questions were asked. The man who hired me was Jack Partington, a producer who put five acts together to make a show – plus a line of chorus girls – that would travel all over the US playing the Paramount theatres.

I was the lowest-paid act on the bill, but at fourteen years old I wasn't arguing. To me, $100 was terrific money.

It was exciting being in show business, with a long contract for security in the most insecure of professions. Yet after a time, the monotony of the shows began to get to me. We played a different city each week. My act had two numbers: 'When Day is Done' and 'I Wanna be Loved by You'. After a couple of days playing those two songs over and over again in each city, I became very tired of them.

Partington had a bright idea for my appearance on stage. I would come out carrying a cumbersome double-bass case, open it, and pull out a cello case. I'd open that, and find a trombone case, then finally – mopping my brow in mock relief – I would find a harmonica case, and there would be my mouth organ.

Hilarious? No – it was a flop.

Then some bright spark thought up a fresh gimmick: I would be a local boy in whichever town we were playing. The master of ceremonies would announce that he had found me crouched outside the stage door shining shoes and playing the mouth organ. (Cries of 'Aaah!')

Each theatre had its own MC. Dick Powell, later to become a screen tough guy in movies like *Johnny O'Clock* and *Cry Danger*, was the resident crooner in Pittsburgh, and proved himself a master at building up the sympathy for poor little me. 'C'mon, folks, give this little kid a great big hand, will ya? What do you say? He's one of our very own, so let's hear you . . .'

I would edge my way on to the stage, twisting myself into contortions of shyness, and hesitantly start to play. I was a skinny kid with large eyes that could look more soulful than a spaniel's, with black curly hair, and when they dressed me in a shabby waistcoat and knickerbockers for my entry, I looked like a waif. To coin a phrase, there wasn't a dry seat in the house. As a local boy, I got more applause than anyone else on the bill.

The only place I didn't try it on was Baltimore, my home town. After all, I *was* a local boy, and I could imagine what my former classmates would do to me if we tried to put that shoeshine boy routine over on them.

Away from the footlights, I was learning fast in other areas. Like sex, for instance. In New Orleans I had my first outing through the red-light district with a tap dancer from the show named Peter.

He stopped to talk to two black girls plying their trade shamelessly on the street. I stood there, totally lost for words. One of the girls pointed to Peter. 'What he do?'

I told her: 'He's a dancer.'

She eyed my small frame up and down with a calculating eye. 'Can you dance?' I shook my head. Without any change of tone, she said: 'Ah kin *fuck*!'

I recoiled so sharply that I hit my head on a lamppost. Until that moment I had never heard a girl swear. Peter gave me a knowing grin, took the hand of his hooker and strolled off into the night, leaving me standing. My own girl gave me a smile that might have been contempt, pity or both, turned her back and walked off, handbag swinging. I just stood there and let her go. Had I carried it further, I really wouldn't have known what to do anyway.

My next adventure was more physical. Considerably more. A month later we were in New York, playing the Paramount Theater in Times Square. After the last show I went round the corner to a late-night eatery called the Horn and Hardart, where I suddenly had an overwhelming desire for cornflakes.

Two girls sitting at a nearby table overhead me, and burst into fits of giggles. 'Little baby wants his cornflakes,' said one, a young blonde with a lot of make-up. 'C'mon over, little baby, and eat your cornflakes.'

Oh boy, it was a pick-up! I was over like a shot, stammered out a few words to introduce myself, and found the girls surprisingly easy to get on with. The blonde was called Marie. They wouldn't let me pay the bill – my first freebie! – but took care of it themselves, and the three of us left together at around two o'clock.

Outside, the other girl waved Marie goodnight, flashed me a knowing smile, and disappeared. The blonde took me round the block to the apartment where she lived, and let me inside. Without a word she undressed. It seemed like a good idea, so I did the same. She climbed into bed, produced a condom from a drawer, and helped me put it on. Again, that was a first. Sadly, the story ends there. Maybe it was the condom. Maybe it was first-night nerves. Either way – nothing.

Marie was very kind, I'll say that for her. She could have made fun of me. Instead she gave me her name and phone number, and asked me to stay in touch.

Next day I called on Nat Brusiloff, who had become a good friend and confidant, and told him what had happened. He took the number from me, and called her. He mumbled a few words into the phone – and fifteen minutes later there was a ring at the bell, and in walked Marie.

Nat poured her a drink, chatted for a few minutes, and then the pair of them disappeared into the bedroom, leaving me feeling like the proverbial spare part. Nat's voice came from the open door: 'Hey, Larry. C'mon in and see this!'

'This' turned out to be their two naked bodies thrashing around on the bed without the slightest hint of embarrassment or shame. I just stood in the doorway, watching in amazement.

After it was over, Nat said: 'Take her home, Larry. Now you know what to do, right?'

Well . . . right. And I did. But there was no real joy or even excitement, because it was just too impersonal and mechanical. In the words of Sammy Kahn's wonderful parody: 'This is my first affair . . . so what goes where?'

But that's how I lost my virginity.

3

Gals, Guns and Gangsters

'Outa my way, kid!'
Al Capone to Larry Adler

'Hey, mister! Just who do you think you are?'
Larry Adler to Al Capone

Chicago in the Roaring Twenties was everything you ever read about, saw on screen, or dreamed of in your wildest imagination – only more. Prohibition was at its peak, ushered in on 16 January 1920 when America was looking the other way, in the direction of World War I, with evangelist Billy Sunday reading the last rites over 'John Barleycorn'.

It never worked. Bar-rooms vanished, but speakeasies erupted – there were 10,000 in Chicago alone, with customers queueing outside armour-plated doors while some gangster's lackey scrutinized them through a grille. If they were let in, it would cost them 20p for a nip of whisky – a huge price – with beer at six times the rate it had been.

At the tender age of fourteen I became part of that raucous, dangerous world. Show business and the underworld rubbed shoulders as if they were old friends – and often they were. Gangsters loved to be part of the scene. Ever wondered why they had names like 'Bedbug' Moran, 'Joe the Bull' Kakadoulis, 'Greasy Thumbs' Gulitz, and the like? It's showbiz, that's why.

That marvellous TV series 'The Untouchables' got it right, with Robert Stack playing cold-eyed Eliot Ness, forever saying: 'Put down the gun, Charlie!' They don't write dialogue like that any more.

In the year of the St Valentine's Day Massacre, 1929, I was still on the road with the variety show, with stop-overs anywhere from Cleveland to Chicago. It was in the latter, the 'windy city', that my big mouth could have cemented a friendship for me – via the river.

We were playing the Oriental Theater for a week. I was squeezed in the middle between the comedy duo of Harry Ross and his partner Eddie Edwards, and an energetic tap dancing team named Ferral and Paul Luis, a sister–brother act who billed themselves as the Tapping Flapper and the Tipping Flipper.

Backstage on the last night, Harry, who also acted as the show's manager, called us together in his dressing-room. He was an ebullient man who had made it his business to take care of me on the road. 'Big night tonight, boys and girls. Party at the Croydon. Make sure you're there – the host doesn't like being stood up.' The Croydon was one of the big hotels in town.

The party was everything a party should be. It was held in the penthouse of the Croydon, the size

of a ballroom, with chandeliers suspended like
glistening teardrops from the ceiling, full-length
mirrors along the walls that doubled the size of the
room, and more than five hundred people dancing
the night away – and drinking illicit hooch from
long tables covered in white cloths at one end.
Champagne and whisky were the order of the night
– that and marijuana, long before the weed became
the trendy thing to inhale in the 1960s.

Marijuana was all the rage. Somewhere in town,
every night, there would be a party, and you would
take along either a bottle or money. I can still feel
that thick, sweet smell in my nostrils – and remember how afraid I was to try it. In fact I neither drank
nor smoked. Even at that tender age I just didn't
want to be out of control.

Wait. I lie. I did smoke a joint once, with Dizzy
Gillespie, but that wouldn't be until the next
decade.

For now, the other kind of joint was jumping. It
was party time, and the casts from every show in
town had been invited. Leggy chorus girls in
skimpy flapper outfits whirled across the floor.
Corks popped. A babble of voices and laughter
filled the room, along with the smoke.

I was at one of the long tables trying to catch the
barman's eye when a burly man with a pallor the
colour of ivory brushed past me. The barman almost
turned somersaults to serve him a drink – of iced
water. I had a vision of a loud waistcoat wrapped
around a beefy middle, a huge cigar stuck in fleshy
lips, eyebrows like black limpets, and a gold ring the

size of a golfball on one finger. He looked at me, and growled amiably: 'Outa my way, kid!'

'Hey, mister,' I rejoined, with all the feckless fervour of a snooty adolescent proving himself in the great big world outside. 'Just who do you think you are?'

The big man paused. A pair of eyes, Sicilian black and brilliant, surveyed me. Then he relaxed, laid a podgy hand on my shoulder, and said: 'You got spunk, kid. How old are you?'

I told him.

'You're a Yid, right?' Some people get down to basics right away.

I couldn't deny it. He looked pleased. 'I thought so. I can always tell. I'm Catholic myself. D'ya go to *shule*?'

No, I said, I didn't go to synagogue.

My new-found inquisitor didn't seem to like that at all. 'Why not?' he demanded.

'Well, we do six shows on a weekend,' I told him. I added that if I had to get up early on Saturdays to go to perform prayer or penance, I wouldn't have enough breath left to climb on the stage, let alone push air through a mouth organ.

He liked that even less. 'Are your parents with you?' No, I said, they're back home in Baltimore.

'But you write to them every day, yeah?'

'Well, no . . . Maybe once every two weeks – '

'How d'ya like that,' growled the big man. 'What kind of kid are you, anyway? This ain't no party for you. Get your coat, go on back to your hotel, sit down and write a letter to your mother and father, OK? *Tonight!'*

'Well, OK, but – '

'No buts. And something else. Next Saturday you're going to *shule*. I don't care how many shows you got to do.'

I nodded dumbly. He gave my shoulder a last powerful squeeze, turned and strode off into the hubbub, acknowledging the guests on all sides. People made way for him as if it was the parting of the Red Sea, then flocked to gather round him like the Egyptians trying to surround the Israelites.

Harry Ross appeared at my elbow, and stared after the burly figure. 'Wow,' he said. 'You know who that was?'

'No,' I said. 'Who *was* that guy?'

'Al Capone,' said Harry, and our complexions turned a whiter shade of pale when I recalled what I'd said to the night's host.

Like so many gangland figures before and since, Capone loved the whole glitzy show-business scene. When he decided to hold a party, every theatre in town would get a blanket invite. And it was generally considered bad for the health not to turn up.

Was this the man who stabbed a guy between the eyes with an ice-pick? The man who cold-bloodedly beat two henchmen to death with a baseball bat at a dinner party because he thought they were infor-mers? I know that in the movie of *The Untouchables*, the film had Robert De Niro killing just one man. In fact there were two. Check the records.

It was time to go. I knew how to take good advice

when I heard it. I made for the door, and found myself passing a group of guests hanging avidly on the words of mine host, who was holding forth in the middle like an actor trying out the soliloquy from *Hamlet*. Al Capone was telling a story. People were transfixed as if it was the second coming.

I paused to listen.

It seemed that one of his 'soldiers' had gunned down a man in broad daylight on State Street, and there were several witnesses prepared to testify. Enough to send Capone's man to the chair on first-degree murder.

'So,' declared Capone, waxing eloquent, 'I had to get to the jury, right?' The acolytes who were clustered around nodded enthusiastically. R-i-i-ight! 'OK, I find a guy, and pay him $25,000 to hold out – not for first-degree murder, but for manslaughter . . . which carried a two- to twenty-year sentence.

'The jury was out for three days. Finally they brought in a verdict of manslaughter. I gave a dinner for the juror, which cost me another few Gs, and said to him: "How did you do it? I never thought you'd get away with manslaughter."

'"Boy!" said the juror. "You don't know what a dumb bunch of bastards I had to put up with. They wanted to *acquit* him!"'

Big Al's corner rocked with laughter. I edged for the door – only to find a large figure I was getting to know quite well looming in front of me, blocking my way.

'Hey,' said Capone. 'Did I tell you? I go to Mass every Sunday, then I buy flowers for my mother.'

A pause. Then: 'Do you send your mother flowers?'

'But she's in Baltimore,' I said, wondering what I'd done to deserve this. 'I told you – '

'So?' rasped Capone. 'You never heard of Western Union? Try wiring them.'

I gave him my best smile, and headed for the door and out of that room. I'd been walking on thin ice for long enough.

I never did see Capone again, though I mixed with other notorious mobsters from those heady Prohibition days. The talk that year was of the St Valentine's Day Massacre, when Al had ordered the execution of seven rival bootleggers in a sleazy Chicago garage. Capone was finally gaoled in 1931 for eleven years for tax evasion. He died on 25 January 1947 after a stroke, aged forty-eight, penniless and wrecked by syphilis, and he was buried in Chicago, in the same graveyard as more than 200 victims of his nefarious business activities.

Yet against all the odds, all the headlines, all the terrifying evidence proving he was a vicious racketeer prone to maniacal psychotic rages, my abiding memory of Scarface Al Capone – incidentally, known to his intimates as Snorkey – is not of a ruthless mobster, but of a man concerned about the religious habits of a fifteen-year-old kid who should have been more caring for his mother.

But then, you can't be right all the time.

The most colourful gangsters of that era had one thing in common: they were all snappy dressers.

Jack 'Legs' Diamond, for instance. He was a sallow-faced man with large stick-out ears who had the unenviable record of having been shot no fewer than seventeen times during his violent career, usually by rival mobsters trying to cash in on his bootlegging activities.

As a result of those seventeen shootings, doctors had removed an incredible thirteen slugs from his body. He showed me a chart published in a magazine in 1931 pinpointing the spots on the 'human target', and he was understandably proud of his record. 'You know, kid,' he said, 'I don't have too many friends.' Indeed, popularity was not a word that twinkled brightly in the Diamond persona.

But sartorially, he was in the top league. He once gave me a piece of advice while we were sitting together at Dave's Blue Room, a New York delicatessen which was a favourite late-night hangout for show folk – and the Mob.

'Never wear a suit costing less than two hundred clams, kid.' In the early 1930s, $200 was like $2,000 today. Three months later 'Legs' would dirty his $200 outfit on the grimy carpet of a rooming house in Dove Street, New York, where they found his body with three bullet holes in the back of his head.

It was in the early hours of a cold December night in 1931 when 'Legs' finally bit his last bullet. His expensive trousers were thrown over a chair, and in a heap on the floor lay his jacket and brown chinchilla coat with the tan soft hat he always wore, with the brim tilted snappily down. It was a gangland execution, ruthlessly and expertly carried out by two men who burst into the second-floor bedroom at 4.30 a.m. to send 'Legs' on his way.

When I heard the news I felt both sick and sad. But, strangely, not frightened – even though I had been rubbing shoulders with this man only days earlier, and had become drawn into the Damon Runyonesque world of gangsters and their molls.

'Legs' had reportedly been a hitman for another legendary gangster and gambler, Arnold Rothstein, whom I first met when I took a British showgirl named Vera Milton to a party he threw at the Park Central Hotel in New York. When Rothstein – known as 'A.R.' to his friends – was eventually shot and killed in his suite in the hotel, the legend was that all the lights in the sign outside went out save for the 'AR' in 'PARK'.

I had quite a crush on Vera. She was a leggy dancer in the Earl Carroll revue *Vanities* at the New Amsterdam Theater in Times Square, where the sign over the door read: THROUGH THESE PORTALS PASS THE MOST BEAUTIFUL GIRLS IN THE WORLD.

We left Rothstein's party at three in the morning, and I hailed a cab, hoping she would invite me back to her place. I was still in my teens – but eager.

'Where to?' I asked.

'Back to the stage door of the New Amsterdam,' she said.

'Vera,' I protested. 'It's three o'clock.'

'I know,' she said. 'Please do as I say.'

We reached the theatre, and I paid off the cab. My heart started to beat a bit faster when I realized: of course, she's taking me into her dressing-room.

But no. Vera marched over to a small car parked up the alley, and rapped on the window. A figure stirred inside, and a bleary face stared through the glass at me.

'Who's that?' I whispered.

'Hubby,' Vera murmured.

Hubby wound down the window and looked at me. He didn't like what he saw. 'This is one hell of a time to be running around the streets with a man,' he growled.

'But darling,' Vera crooned. 'It's not a *man* – it's *Larry*!'

The mobsters liked me because I was showbiz. I was also unique to them – a skinny kid of seventeen who was able to coax the kind of sounds out of a mouth organ they had never heard before. So I was accepted. But in my ignorance I nearly fell foul of 'Legs' himself, without ever realizing it.

In 1931 my manager Gus Edwards got me an audition for a musical that was being staged by the legendary Florenz Ziegfeld. It was called *Smiles*, and was about a Salvation Army lass who Does Good, and brings a smile wherever she sets her dainty foot. Fred Astaire and his sister Adele were in it, along with Eddie Foy Jnr.

The big draw was Marilyn Miller, one of the celebrated stars of Broadway musicals in the 1920s, who had been on stage from the age of five and, as far as I could see, had never lost her childish temperament.

I had a solo number entitled 'I'm Glad I Waited', which turned out to be a show-stopper. Ziegfeld

was happy. Gus Edwards was happy. I was happy
– until Ziegfeld asked me to replace it with a ballad
that Marilyn was singing. I stuck out for my song.

'Mr Ziegfeld, you're the boss. If you want me to
change my solo, I'll have to. But it stops the show
every night. And that other one – it's pretty dreary.'

'Suit yourself,' said Ziegfeld, who always seemed
to have his mind on other things.

The ballad I rejected was 'Time on My Hands',
which, as the world knows, is pretty dreary!

But what really brought a smile to my face was a
chorus girl called Marion Roberts, a dancer with a
mop of dark hair, the most seductive eyes this side
of the Hudson River, and the kind of earthy beauty
you find in Eastern European women. Perhaps her
real name, Marion Strasmick, had its origins in
Poland. We all called her Kiki.

All I know is that I had the most enormous crush
on this girl. To me she had a virginal, almost
ethereal beauty and a shyness that brought out the
protector in me. That was me, a seventeen-year-old
minder.

She trusted me, too, possibly because she knew
I was no threat. In Boston, after we opened at the
Shubert Theater on the pre-run to Broadway, we
had a late supper after the show every night. I
walked her back to our hotel, gave her a peck on
the cheek, and wished her goodnight. I never made
a pass, because it would have been sacrilege to
defile that sweet young innocent girl.

When the show came to New York, I became
even more protective, though somehow I didn't see

her as much as I'd have liked in the hurly-burly of
Broadway. I felt it was my duty to keep her away
from the stage-door Johnnies and the wolves prowl-
ing the streets of Manhattan.

In short, I had what is known in impolite society
as 'the hots' for this chorine, though I would never
stoop to revealing it to my love goddess.

There was one problem. So had 'Legs' Diamond
. . . but nobody told me.

She had met him at a nightclub where she went
with some friends after the show. He ordered
champagne for the entire party, drove her home
that night, and asked permission to phone her.
'Legs' was flamboyant, and he had style. He sent
nightly telegrams to the Ziegfeld Theater to tell her
where they were having dinner after the show.
Much later, after his death, she would insist that she
never saw a gangster or a gun while they were
together.

The first I knew of it was when I saw a headline
emblazoned in two-inch type across the front page of
the *Graphic*: 'LEGS' SHOT IN CHORINE'S BED. Don't ask me
how, but I knew before I bought the paper who the
chorine was going to be. Kiki had been Diamond's
mistress for months, and I never knew it.

This was one of the seventeen near-misses. 'Legs'
had been shot through the door of his apartment
while he was in bed with Marion. He wasn't
seriously hurt, but it must have been a heck of a
shock. Marion never showed up again in *Smiles*, and
I drowned my sorrows in lemonade – if not older,
then sadder and suddenly wiser.

Five years later I was in a Greenwich Village bar. I heard my name called by a lady sitting on a bar stool. Her voice was slurred. 'Larree ... *Lar-ree!*' I walked across to her, and peered into a face that had once been beautiful but was now ravaged and drawn. A face I knew. It was Marion, and she was drunk. Very drunk.

'I'll never forget you, kiddo,' she said. 'You're the only one ever treated me like a fuckin' lady.' I could have wept.

Another useful piece of advice came from Bugsy Siegel, who carved his name in infamy by running the gambling rackets in Las Vegas before coming to a sticky end on 20 June 1947 at the Moorish-style Beverly Hills mansion at No. 810, North Lincoln Drive owned by his 'secret wife' Virginia Hill.

I actually heard the shots that killed him. I was just a couple of short blocks away at No. 609, and thought it was a car back-firing. In fact it was a Mafia hitman armed with a 30-30 carbine pumping steel-coated bullets into Bugsy through the ground-floor window, while the one-time reputed West Coast chief of Murder Inc. was sitting on the sofa reading the local paper.

Bugsy's 'crime'? He had been skimming the profits from the gambling tables in Vegas and stashing them in his personal Swiss bank account. The Mob warned him, but he ignored them. And paid with his life, at the age of forty-two.

A month before, I had been playing at the

Flamingo in Las Vegas. That's the hotel on the famous neon strip that had been built by Bugsy with $1 million of his own money and a further $5 million belonging to the Mafia.

I was sitting with him over a coffee in the lounge late one night. The show was over. It had been a good one. Now I was relaxing. I studied the man next to me, a man reputedly with so much blood on his hands.

In the flesh Benjamin 'Bugsy' Siegel had the air of a movie star. With his chiselled looks and baby-blue eyes, he could charm the paper off a wall. Warren Beatty got it right in the film *Bugsy* – the charisma, the arrogance, the sheer effrontery that would eventually be his undoing. I saw a taste of it that night.

All of a sudden Bugsy asked: 'Are you a gambling man, Larry?'

'No, Mr Siegel,' I replied – no one ever called him 'Bugsy' to his face. 'I'm not.'

'Let me give you a tip anyway,' he said. 'Never bet unless you're sure you're going to win.'

I frowned. 'Mr Siegel – how can you be sure you're going to win unless the bet is fixed?'

He smiled broadly. 'You're learning, kid!' he said.

The next night he was at his usual table, and beckoned me over. 'Sit down,' he said. 'Remember what we were talking about last night?'

I nodded.

'Watch this, kid! How to make twenty grand the easy way – '

He looked past me to the carpeted entrance, and

waved at someone. 'Hey, Sam!' A middle-aged man in an expensive suit came over.

Bugsy, exuding bonhomie, rose and pumped his hand. 'Come and join us for a drink. Sam, meet Larry. Larry, this is Sam, one of our high rollers.'

I couldn't help noticing Sam's diamond cufflinks – they were flashing like a lighthouse on a dark night. His tie-pin, too. And his watch. He appeared overwhelmed to be invited to join the great Bugsy Siegel, undisputed king of Vegas, and willingly sat down.

'You're a betting man, aren't you?' Bugsy inquired.

'Yeah, sure I am.'

'OK.' Bugsy fished into the sugar bowl, and produced two lumps of white sugar. He put one in front of the newcomer, the other in front of himself. Then he said: 'I'll bet you ten grand that a fly lands on your lump of sugar before mine.'

There was a brief silence. Then the other man nodded. 'OK, it's an even money bet. Ten grand it is.'

We sat in an uneasy silence for forty-five minutes. I'd done my show, and had no place to go except bed. But I suspected it would be unwise even to go to the bathroom.

Finally a fly buzzed around the table, completed a few circles above our unmoving heads – and settled on the newcomer's lump of sugar.

Sam kept his features commendably impassive, thought for a moment, then – as Bugsy knew he would – said: 'Double or nothing?'

'Sure,' said Bugsy. 'But let's make it fair.'

He took the lumps of sugar and swapped them over, then sat back and folded his hands across his waistcoat. This time it was only ten minutes before another fly – or maybe the same one with a sweet tooth – buzzed up, had a look . . . and landed smack on the other guy's sugar. Siegel had won $20,000.

Sam sighed, fished in his pocket and pulled out a slip of paper. His marker. He signed the IOU, rose and shook hands and headed for the tables in the casino outside. Bugsy winked at me. 'How about that?' he said. 'Wanna know how I did it?'

I shook my head in amazement. 'Unbelievable,' I said. 'How can you gamble on a *fly*?'

'Easy,' he said. And explained how he had prepared two lumps of sugar with camphor on one side. Camphor is a repellant. When he first put the sugar down, his lump had camphor on the upper side, and there was no chance of a fly landing on it. The other lump he had doctored had the camphor on the underside. When he swapped them, he simply turned the lumps over.

That was Bugsy. Clever – but in the end, too clever for his own health.

OK, they said it was the Mob that rubbed him out. My guess is that someone told the guy with the lump of sugar how that fly trick was done.

Meyer Lansky, another legendary Mafia figure I met in Florida, could have saved Bugsy. This man was one of the dons, a Jewish racketeer from New York who was the inspiration for the character of Hyman Roth in *Godfather 2*, and variously known as Chairman of the Board and Underworld Big Shot – and quoted as saying his slice of organized crime was 'bigger than US Steel', meaning a personal wealth of $300 million. A figure I always felt was somewhat exaggerated, but at least Lansky was one of the few to die peacefully in his bed, in 1983, at the considerable age of eighty-one.

Bugsy Siegel had been his protégé, groomed to take his place in the Mob hierarchy. I had been playing at a club in one of the condominiums in Miami, where Lansky had retreated to carry on his operation in the Florida sunshine.

On my first night he came hobbling up to me on two canes, a small man with a pouchy face and a wide hair parting in the middle.

'Nice show,' he said. Then: 'You don't recognize me, do you?'

'Should I?' I inquired, not wishing to offend.

'Ask around,' said Lansky. 'Just ask around.' And off he shuffled. He was the only Jewish gangster ever to hold a top position in the Mafia, and I would see him walking slowly along the street with his fox terrier skipping around him on the end of a long leash, and no sign of a bodyguard. No car following him. Nobody shadowing him.

Some people got away with it.

Like I say, gangsters were all crazy about show business. Several of them put money into shows so that they could be near the action – and near the chorus girls who went with the action. I often wonder how many productions were launched on a tide of alcohol from the illicit stills and illegal clubs you could find down any back street in any city – if you knew where to look.

Violence was only a breath away from the veneer of bonhomie and back-slapping that would herald the appearance of a mobster in our midst. I was aware of it, and was usually able to keep my distance from trouble. But there was one moment that brought vividly home to me just how thin the ice really was on which I was treading.

The show was *Flying Colors*, the first musical to present a racially mixed chorus. A number called 'Bless the Butler' featured a black comedienne named Billie Worth, and on opening night in Philadelphia the audience rose to her when she stepped out of an otherwise white chorus line and simply walked away with the number.

Many of the cast would go on to great things: the tall, elegant Clifton Webb, wise-cracking funny lady Patsy Kelly, whose deadpan comedy style persuaded Hal Roach to take her to Hollywood to kick off a glittering movie career, and Buddy Ebsen, who would later strike it rich as the head of the Beverly Hillbillies clan in the 1960s TV series.

Me, I played a mouth organ solo of 'Alone Together', thumped the keys of a dummy piano, and drove a team of horses in 'Louisiana Hayride', with a marvellous back-projection that made it look as if I was on a real waggon rolling down a real country road. It got a cheer every night.

One of the show's backers was 'Waxey' Gordon, real name Joseph Wechsler, a notorious gangland figure who looked and acted the role to frightening perfection. He was a nasty, unpredictable piece of work, and I was advised to avoid him as far as possible. He threw an opening-night party after the show, and we all gathered in the penthouse of the Hotel Warwick with the lights of Philadelphia spread out below.

At the time I had a girlfriend named Sally, a brunette model who had been on the cover of *College Humor* and had a cool authority about her that was unusual. She lived in New York, and I invited her to take the train down to see the opening night, and come on with me to the party afterwards.

It was a typically lavish spread, with champagne flowing, canapes brought around by waiters, and at the far end of the room a live group thumping out numbers from the show.

'Waxey' appeared beside us. Close to, I could see how he got his nickname: the pallor of his skin was the colour of death.

'You're the kid with the tin sandwich,' he said, without preamble. Then he looked at my companion. 'Who's she?'

I introduced him to Sally, and he eyed her up and down, taking his time. 'Hmm!' he said. 'Nice.' And he turned on his heel and walked away.

Sally shivered. 'What a dreadful man,' she said.

'Yes,' I told her gently. 'But he's one of the

backers. We're stuck with him. But we don't have to talk to him.'

Ten minutes later there was a tap on my shoulder. Sally had gone to the powder room. A dark man with a thin face, dressed in a loud striped suit, black shirt and white tie, scowled at me.

I recognised him. Johnny "Ice" Chisholm, Waxey's bodyguard. 'Waxey says: beat it. Gowwan – get out of here. Screw!'

I gulped. I have never thought of myself as courageous – a card-carrying coward, that's me. Even at that comparatively tender age I knew better than to argue, but I wasn't going to leave Sally with those jerks.

Instead I nodded at him, and made for the door. Sally was just coming through it. I grabbed her arm. 'Get your coat,' I said tersely. 'We're leaving.'

I didn't look back, but as we walked out to the lift along the corridor, my shoulderblades were tingling. Believe me, I genuinely expected a bullet or a knife in the back. It was the longest walk of my young life, and I can still see the colour of the carpet. Yellow.

Symbolic? Not really. I still rate it among the bravest, or perhaps most foolish, acts I ever did. As for 'Waxey' – he never mentioned it again.

I often wondered whether the gangsters I was hob-nobbing with were carrying guns, or 'packing a piece', as local parlance had it. If they were, I never saw any sign of it, and somehow I didn't like to ask. In fact the only two times in my life I saw a pistol both involved women, and both times the guns were being pointed at my head.

I started young – with guns *and* gals. I was fifteen when I met Dorothy Fox, a girl with all the right curves in all the right places. I took her out for almost a year, and though I wasn't earning too much money I could still behave like a high roller, taking her to all the expensive places in New York.

How? Simple. In those days the hotels and clubs put on regular 'Celebrity Nights', advertising them widely to tempt in the public. The idea was that a celebrity would get up from his table, march out on to the stage or dance floor, and do a number. In return, he wasn't given a bill. No money exchanged hands – either way.

This suited me down to the ground. Already I was making a few waves on the showbiz front, and my name was starting to be bandied around. People were getting to know me. I was also able to show the club owners programmes from the theatres or variety halls where I was appearing.

Presto! I was able to eat, drink and be merry, strictly *gratis*, and impress Dorothy at the sam time. She never knew we were getting it all for free, and frequently we would hit the town and take in more than one place in a night. The St Moritz Roof and the Central Park Casino, where the pianist was Eddy Duchin, were two of my regular favourites. I would tip the wink to the MC, and would always be called up to play a number. Quite often I didn't get Dorothy home until three in the morning.

She was a flirtatious girl who only wanted a good

time – and I was able to give her one, if you'll forgive the ambiguity. She came from a wealthy family, and one day she called me from their summer home on Long Island at a place called Neponset. Would I like to come out for the weekend?

Would I? Those houses were million-dollar mansions, and I wasn't going to stand up a chance of moving in high society for a couple of days.

I took the train out from Grand Central, and was met at the station by the family limousine, with a chauffeur attached. He drove me in silence along the coast road to an imposing edifice facing the ocean. Dorothy greeted me, and seemed a trifle strained. I'd met her folks before, and got on well enough with them. But this time I sensed an atmosphere as we sat down to lunch. Somehow they seemed somewhat less cordial than usual.

After lunch Mr Fox said: 'Shall we go for a drive, Larry?' He was a burly, silver-haired businessman with the air of someone who was used to giving orders rather than taking them.

'Why sure, sir. That would be nice.'

I sat up front with the chauffeur. Dorothy and her father sat in the back. We headed out into the ocean drive. After half a mile her dad ordered the chauffeur to turn right along a winding road with big trees that sent dark shadows slanting over the sun-dappled tarmac. There was no one else around, no traffic, nobody. 'Slow down, but keep going,' he said.

Suddenly I felt something cold and hard pressed

behind my right ear. I froze. Dorothy's father said quietly: 'Turn round, Larry!'

I turned – and stared straight into the muzzle of a pistol three inches from my nose. My mouth dropped open. 'What – what's that for?' Stupid question, really, but right then I couldn't think of anything wittier.

Mr Fox fixed me with a gaze every bit as chilly as the gun he held in an unwavering hand. 'Dorothy is pregnant,' he said.

'What! Oh no.'

'Oh yes.'

I started to stutter. 'Well . . . why point that gun at me? Please, put it away.' Throughout all this, the chauffeur kept his eyes on the road. I caught myself wondering if his boss made a habit of waving a gun around.

'Look, sir,' I went on hurriedly. 'If that's the case, of course I'll marry her.' I looked at Dorothy. Her eyes were bright and shining – with young love or gratitude, I couldn't tell. Maybe both.

'Dorothy,' said Mr Fox heavily, 'is fourteen years old.'

Christ, I thought! Fourteen! All those nights on the town – and in bed! I'd had no idea. The girl possessed the body of a young woman – built for loving, as I would tell her in our tender moments together. I was thunderstruck . . . and in trouble.

'What – what's going to happen?' I asked finally.

Mr Fox slowly removed the gun from my nostrils, and tucked it away in his pocket. 'I guess we'll just wait and see,' he said.

I took the next train back to the big city.

Several sleepless nights later, the phone rang. Dorothy's voice. 'It's OK, Larry. I'm not pregnant after all. And Mom and Dad say we can go on seeing each other!'

We did, too. But from then on, we were a lot more careful. As for Mom and Dad's attitude – life is full of surprises.

The other time I found myself on the wrong end of a gun happened in the 1950s. I was playing in St Louis, the star of my own show, and I had given several interviews to the papers and radio stations. People knew I was in town.

So I wasn't particularly surprised when the phone rang in my suite at the Chase Hotel, and a female voice said: 'Mr Adler, I'm in the foyer, and I'm here to raise funds for charity. I wonder if you could spare me a few minutes.'

Without thinking, I said: 'Sure, come on up.' I should have gone downstairs to meet her on neutral ground, but she sounded genuine enough.

A tap at the door, and there stood an attractive young woman of about twenty-three, with long jet-black hair and a nervous smile. 'Come on in, honey,' I said, to make her feel at ease. The one slightly disturbing note was that she had taken very little trouble over her appearance. She was sloppily dressed, in faded jeans and a shabby jacket – not the sort of person you expect to find wandering around a five-star hotel.

'Which charity are you talking about?' I inquired, gesturing her to a chair. She remained standing.

Then suddenly, startlingly, she burst out: 'I am raising money for the Irgun. Give me anything you can!'

The Irgun was the name of a Zionist terror group. I stared at her, astounded. 'Look, I hope that Palestine does become an Israeli state, and I can see what you're doing. But they're a terrorist gang. I'm not going to pay a single cent towards them – '

While I was in the middle of my brief homily, she began to fish around in the pocket of her jacket. She pulled out a Beretta, the kind that James Bond was already making famous, and pointed it at me. Her hand was shaking. So was I – afterwards. At the time I was more taken aback than scared.

'Honey,' I said. 'What are you *doing*?'

Her voice rose to a shout. *'You're our enemy! You must die!'*

It's funny (funny-strange, not funny-ha ha) how you react when confronted with what is a potentially deadly situation. In this case, a deranged woman with a gun that was waving all over the place, but mostly in my direction. I could have dived behind the sofa, or made a run for the door.

Instead, in the tones of a schoolmaster admonishing a fractious pupil, I said crossly: 'Oh, don't be so dramatic!' And I edged towards her until I was only a foot away, keeping my eyes locked into hers, trying to ignore the gun – until I could reach out and ever so gently take the pistol out of her grasp. She didn't try to resist. More important, she didn't pull the trigger. Instead she burst into tears and, sobbing loudly, ran out of the room and out of sight.

Staring blankly down at the Beretta in my hand, I just hoped the hotel detective wasn't patrolling the corridor at that particular moment. He wasn't. I should have called the police, but I never did get round to it.

What happened to the gun? I tucked it away in the bottom of my suitcase, and took it with me when I went back home to Los Angeles. There I put it in the back of a drawer, and forgot all about it.

When I came to move house a year later, somehow it had disappeared. Maybe the cleaning lady took it, but I never got round to asking her.

If you saw *Guys and Dolls*, you will realize the kind of world I was mixing with. That included the man who observed it, relished it, and wrote it down for posterity. Damon Runyon was small and dapper, with sharp pale-blue eyes behind wire-rimmed glasses. He always wore a hat, and sported a white carnation in his buttonhole. The only place I didn't see him wear that hat was the Stork Club in New York, and then only because they wouldn't let him.

His cronies were men like Walter Winchell, Sidney Skolsky, Leonard Lyons and other luminaries of the fourth estate. Runyon would listen to the colourful stories flowing around the tables, often embellished or merely economical with the truth, and make notes in a little pad he kept in his pocket.

Winchell, of course, was the feared gossip writer whose daily syndicated column made him the most

powerful showbiz journalist in the land, from Hollywood to New York and back. He was very
aggressive, with a firm belief that he was God. That
marvellous movie *The Sweet Smell of Success* was
based on his power play, though in fact Burt
Lancaster looked nothing like him.

The other mistake in the script was that he had his
favourite table at the 21 Club. But Winchell was never
allowed into the 21 – he was a vicious columnist, and
the owners didn't want their clients to get nervous
of bad publicity. So Walter was banned.

He was friendly enough to me in the early days.
But once I got into political trouble and became
caught up in the infamous McCarthy witch-hunt, he
changed. Almost overnight his pen was leaking
vitriol all over me.

Skolsky was a columnist for the New York *Daily
News*, Lyons wrote for the *New York Post*. They were
a lively bunch, characters every one of them, and I
would hang out with them at clubs like Dave's Blue
Room and Lindy's – later made famous by Runyon
as 'Mindy's' – which were the haunt of showbiz
folk, the Mob and the sporting gentry.

Runyon created a whole new language with those
evocative stories he wrote. I still wonder where he
got it from – not from his notebook, that's for sure,
because none of those guys ever spoke like that!
Certainly not in my hearing, anyway. Sure they
were flamboyant, arrogant, and did an awful lot of
talking, but I suspect Runyon overheard what they
were saying, wrote it all down, then simply trans-
ferred it into his own unique idiom.

The downside was that he was a notoriously mean man. He seemed to have domestic problems – he once told me how his children hated him. Why, I never found out. But in all the years we ate, drank and laughed together I never once saw him reach for his wallet. Nor was he ever presented with a bill. So who knows? Perhaps he didn't have to.

As his fame grew, Runyon became the natural target for the figures on the shady side of the street who frequented those establishments. Not a night would go by without maybe half a dozen figures in double-breasted suits and loud ties greeting him like a long-lost brother as they passed his table. Since a drink would inevitably follow, Runyon was only too happy to respond to their fraternal fellowship.

Sometimes I would be introduced, other times not. One night we were sitting, just the two of us, at his usual table in the inner room at the Stork Club – a room reserved for VIPs – when a man came up and without invitation plumped himself down into the chair next to him. He leaned forward, and for several minutes muttered in Damon's ear. The writer nodded, listened intently, frowned, nodded again. Finally the fellow got up and walked away. He hadn't looked at me once.

'What was all that about?' I asked.

Runyon said: 'I didn't want to embarrass you. That guy just got out of Sing-Sing today. He'd murdered his wife and three kids, beaten the chair, done his sentence, and wanted to tell me all about it.' He paused, then leaned forward and added softly: 'You've just got to go along with a guy like that.'

Some years later I was back at that same table. This time Walter Winchell, Leonard Lyons and a famous theatrical agent named Paul Small were with us. Damon Runyon had been suffering from throat cancer, and after an operation he was now forced to write on a pad anything he wanted to say.

The rest of us were getting into one of those vociferous debates that so often end in a heated argument, usually over the fifth whisky. I wasn't drinking. But for some reason I had climbed on to an invisible soapbox and was behaving like a leather-lunged orator at Hyde Park Corner.

The subject was: Harold Arlen, Cole Porter, Jerome Kern, George Gershwin, and their various attributes, talents, virtues and limitations. Someone mentioned Irving Berlin, and that did it.

'Berlin?' I cried. 'He isn't in the same league. I tell you, I can sit at a piano and improvise, playing whatever comes into my head. I can go on for two hours – and I'll bet you here and now that in all that time I wouldn't play *one* Berlin tune.'

At this point Runyon took out his pad, and carefully wrote something on it. This he passed to Leonard, who let out a bellow of laughter. On to Paul Small, same reaction. It got to Winchell, who nearly fell off his chair.

'Come on,' I said. 'Let's see it.'

Walter passed the pad to me. Runyon had written two words. *'Poor Irving!'*

Damon Runyon could be very cruel sometimes.

He died in 1946 at the age of sixty-six, after an agonizing battle with his cancer, and never did get to see the tumultuous reception for the musical *Guys and Dolls* two years afterwards. His ashes were scattered over Broadway on 18 December 1946 from a plane flown by his life-long friend Captain Eddie Rickenbacker, the American World War I air ace.

George Raft was the closest Hollywood came to getting it right. I'm talking about gangsters. Edward G. Robinson had a great snarl. James Cagney made it to the 'top of the world, Ma!' They are the stuff of screen legend, and deserve it.

But for me, George had that extra something, that indefinable menace that was all the more terrifying because he hardly ever raised his voice. Maybe it was because he saw the real thing in the clubs we both frequented that gave him the edge. Maybe it was growing up in Hell's Kitchen where he was a member of a street gang, and once described himself as: 'young, ambitious and tough, driving Owney Madden's bullet-proof sedan or delivering a load of bootleg booze to Dutch Schultz'.

Reminiscing on those days with me, he recalled with a wry grin: 'I had a gun in my pocket and I was cocky because I was working for the gang boss of New York.'

George was twenty years older than me, a prize-fighter who changed his footwork to become a ballroom dancer before moving into the glitz of nightclubs and Broadway shows. The zenith of this part of his career was when he achieved a reputation as the world's fastest Charleston dancer.

But it was his other image that took him to the
top: his role as the coin-flipping Guido Rinaldo in
Scarface in 1932 established him as one of the
screen's great gangsters. In all, George would make
106 films, and leave eighty-seven of them feet first.

When I finally made it myself to Hollywood, and
was filming *The Singing Marine* at Warner Bros, I
bumped into Raft again in the studio restaurant. He
had made that coin flipping his trademark, and I
couldn't help asking: 'George, I've always
wondered why that coin trick caught on with the
public. It's so easy to do.'

'*Without looking at it?*' said George, in that voice
like someone walking over a shingle beach. 'You
try it!'

He was right. In *Scarface* he had bestowed that
scary snake-eyed stare on people while the coin
went up and down, up and down. Very effective. It
must have been to have been fixed indelibly in our
minds all these years.

I only saw George drop that coin once. It was at
a Royal Variety Show at the London Palladium. The
drapes were down. The stage was empty between
acts. Suddenly, unbilled, unheralded and
unexpected, George Raft strolled out on to the
stage.

There were cries of recognition, and a burst of
applause. He just stood there, staring out at the
audience, expressionless, waiting for the clapping
to die down.

When it finally subsided he fished into his
pocket, pulled out a coin, flipped it into the air –

and missed! The coin rolled noisily away into the footlights. George snapped his fingers in irritation. '*Damn!*' that gesture said. And he walked off. He never said a word, and he didn't come back for the finale. But the roars of laughter followed him into the wings and out into the street.

Capone liked *Scarface* very much, even though by then he was incarcerated in Cook County Jail and the subtitle to the film was *The Shame of a Nation*. When the word went out that Al was pleased, George Raft's standing with the Mob soared sky-high. Paul Muni had given the performance of his life in the lead role, and Howard Hawks's direction was pulsating and true to life (and death).

George found himself stuck with his new image. 'I lost count of the number of ways I got killed off,' he moaned once. 'But the way I went out in *Scarface* was the most dramatic – for me. I got shot, of course. But my head went back so hard I hit a door and nearly knocked myself out. They told me afterwards my eyes went rolling about my head as if they were on separate pivots – but I don't remember a thing about it.'

George had his little foibles. Friends who called at his home in Beverly Hills, with its three bedrooms and kidney-shaped pool, would not be surprised to find him preparing to go out, immaculate in starched white shirt monogrammed with his initials, sober tie with a double Windsor knot, and his small feet encased in polished black shoes, as befitted someone who regularly found himself in the top ten list of best-dressed men. All that would be missing were the trousers.

'Don't worry,' George would assure them. 'My memory ain't that bad. I like to keep my trousers pressed until the minute I walk out of the front door.'

The last time we met I was about to make a picture for Paramount. We sat together at a baseball game in New York on the night before I was due to fly to Hollywood. George growled: 'Let me know if they give you a hard time, and I'll beat the shit out of them!' He gave me a sideways look. I didn't know if he was being half-serious. Or a quarter-serious. Or – well, serious.

George once confessed that he had spent over a million dollars on women. I believed him. He finally died of asthma in a modest bachelor apartment where he lived alone on the seventh floor on the fringe of downtown Los Angeles.

Raft had been banned from re-entering Britain because – as 'front man' for the Colony Club in Berkely Square – it was felt he was bringing the wrong kind of glamour to the casinos and the type of people who operated them. The sad thing is that he would have lived longer in the English climate that was better for his chest than the dry dusty streets of LA. Or so he said.

But that was George Raft, and I liked him. A man who too often found himself in bad company for his own good.

4

Hollywood and Bust!

'Man, you don't play that fuckin' thing –
you sing *it!'*

Billie Holiday

It was when I saw Cary Grant locked in a passionate embrace on a mattress with Randolph Scott, both of them wearing only swimming trunks, that I really felt I had arrived in Hollywood. I mean, I must have been accepted, for these two stalwarts of the box-office – one the leading romantic hero of his day, the other a craggy survivor of countless Western shoot-outs – to behave like that in front of me without a care in the world.

In fact, not just me – but in front of two dozen others at a weekend party at Randy's beach house in Malibu.

By then, I was part of the in-crowd. Invited to all the 'A' parties – they're the ones that take place in million-dollar mansions in Bel-Air, Beverly Hills and Malibu. Hobnobbing with studio chiefs. Swapping jokes with stars and top agents around the pools of the very rich and very famous.

My harmonica, my trusty – not rusty – friend, was always invited along too, just in case I should feel in the mood to blow a few informal notes and liven up the party.

This occasion was a glorious summer's day. Fish were jumping, and the surf – if not the cotton – was high. Familiar faces like James Stewart, Ginger Rogers and Fred and Adele Astaire gathered to sip champagne on Randolph Scott's patio looking out on to the foaming Pacific surf.

Randy had phoned to invite me over. 'It's all very informal, Larry, just a few friends. But do bring your harmonica, won't you?'

To be honest, I never did like putting on a show when it was taken for granted that I would do so. I still don't. Very seldom do I play at parties, though I take my little friend along in my pocket in case the occasion lends itself and I get in the mood. Otherwise – sorry, but no dice.

Randy greeted me at the door of his beach house, a rambling wooden bungalow, beautifully furnished with thick rugs, a bar, picture windows overlooking the ocean, and various trophies from his movies decorating the walls and shelves. An amiable man with the kind of face that you expect to be hewn out of solid Arizona rock, he was startlingly clad in a pair of purple swimming trunks. But at fifty, he still had a fine physique and sported a great tan. All that was missing was the white Stetson.

I knew him like we all know him: tall and rugged, the weather-beaten star of innumerable sage-brush sagas with titles like *Colt .45*, *The Caribou Trail*, *Man in the Saddle*, or *Riding Shotgun* where he always wore the white hat and won the final duel on Main Street. In fact it was Lee Marvin who gave Randy credit for his favourite death scene.

'We were out there in the street,' he told me. 'And I was the fastest gun in the West – as usual, I was wearing the black hat.

'I face Randy, we circle each other slowly with the tension building, and then – wham! We go for the draw. Somehow we have to show how fast he is, and I came up with a great idea.

'I go for my guns, draw – and then look down in disbelief as he shoots me. Empty hands! That's right – I couldn't even get to my holsters. That's how fast he was. It worked a treat. I've been killed off more than seventy times in films, but that always remained my most memorable moment.'

My own most memorable moment featuring Randolph Scott was about to take place on the floor of his living-room. The party was in full swing. Cary Grant, an old friend and partner – in the Members' Stand – at Wimbledon, greeted me jovially. Like a lot of the guests, he too was in a costume – several of them had been for a dip in the ocean to work up an appetite for the buffet lunch that was laid out around the polished driftwood table in the dining-room.

I was never a great drinker, though by now I had acquired a taste for champagne, and I could manage a glass of white wine happily enough. I took an orange juice. The rest of the party was getting noisy.

I wandered out on to the patio, exchanged

greetings with my old pal Fred Astaire and his lovely sister, and after a few minutes headed back inside.

That was when I stopped dead in my tracks as I saw the two figures in front of me.

There were Cary Grant and Randolph Scott lying on a thick white rug by the far window, hugging and stroking each other and giggling like two love birds who hadn't seen each other in years and had a lot of ground to make up. If their fans could see them now, I thought, heading for the bar and for once pouring myself a stiff drink to get over the shock.

And I *was* shaken, I can tell you. I knew about Grant's homosexual tendencies, always latent in him despite his four failed marriages – to actress Virginia Cherrill, heiress Barbara Hutton, and actresses Betsy Drake and Dyan Cannon.

But Randolph Scott! Wow!

They weren't camping it up, either, as I found out later when I made a few inquiries of my fellow guests. They just adored each other . . .

Strangely, there was nothing vulgar about it. And certainly not discreet, either. They just ignored everyone else and threshed around on that rug, until a butler appeared in the doorway and without batting an eyelid announced: 'Luncheon is served. This way, please.'

Maybe Lee Marvin got away lucky. Or Scott-free.

The sexual machinations – and deviations – rampant in Hollywood always astounded me. You want a for-instance? When I heard that the wonderful sophisticated comedienne Claudette Colbert was a strident leader of the lesbian fraternity – or should that be sorority? – along with her close friend Kay Francis, it shattered a whole load of my naïve illusions. I grew up, fast.

I had made my own Hollywood debut in a film that never was – well, not for me. By 1934 I had been taken on by the prestigious William Morris agency, largely on the strength of my harmonica act and the big names with whom I appeared. Duke Ellington, Count Basie, Django Reinhardt, Dizzy Gillespie, Hoagy Carmichael, and the other jazz kings of that brilliant foot-tapping era – I shared the stage with all of them.

It was Dizzy, in fact, who persuaded me into something I had never tried before, or since: to smoke marijuana. Even when I was a kid in the business, all my elders and so-called betters attempted to get me to take dope and drink. But I was made of stern stuff, and always managed to talk my way out of it. I just didn't want either a foreign chemical in my body, or to lose control.

Until one night in 1959, when I was older, and should have known better. Dizzy turned up at my show in Chicago, when I was top of the bill and pulling in full houses. Afterwards he came backstage, sat down and chatted away until I had changed out of my outfit and was ready to go.

'Hey,' he said suddenly. 'You wanna smoke something, Larry?'

I didn't. But for some reason it felt churlish to

refuse. We went back to my hotel room, and I saw him filling a pipe with what looked like tobacco. He handed it to me – but omitted to inform me how the stuff should be smoked.

I puffed happily away at the pipe. After thirty minutes, I was gone! All I can say is that if I had been asked to do a show I could not have put one note after another. On the other hand, I might have given the greatest concert ever – though I doubt it. I never tried it again.

Next night he was back at the theatre. Without warning he strolled out on to the stage, and we played a duet of 'My Man' together. When it was over, he flung his arms around me and kissed me. Dizzy was *very* gay.

'Man,' he said, into the microphone. 'We've just *gotta* make a marriage together.'

I recoiled, but not too obviously. 'Dizzy,' I told him severely, 'you must know that mixed marriages never work!'

Sometimes you have to be fast on your verbal feet.

Back to the movie that never was. The William Morris agency signed me to do a film called *Operator 13*, a pot-boiler about an actress (Marion Davies) who becomes a Union spy during the Civil War.

The lead was Gary Cooper, and I would be in there alongside him playing some marvellous Stephen Foster melodies from the Deep South. Or so I thought. The movie took months to be put together, in that process known as 'pre-production'. In this case, it was more like a massacre. People were fired, among them the producer Walter Wanger and the director Raoul Walsh. Others were hired. Just before shooting started the casting director, who rejoiced in the name of Ben Piazza, called me into his office.

'Change of plan,' he said. 'We're going to find some little black boy to mime to your music, but it'll be you on the soundtrack.'

'No way,' I said – or words to that effect. I wanted the world to see my handsome features on celluloid.

'Kid,' said the casting director. 'You're not taking the right attitude.'

The good news was that I drew a salary for twenty weeks without playing a note. The bad news was that after the minor fracas with the casting director, Larry Adler was taken off the payroll.

When the film was finally made – with two new names in the hot seat (Lucien Hubbard, producer, and Richard Boleslawski, director) there were no folk songs – and no mouth organ, either.

I told you I had *chutzpah*, right? I got my foot into the door in Hollywood through a piece of classic cheek. In 1933 I was appearing at the Chicago Theater on a four-week tour, when I read in *Variety* that the world-famous Grauman's Chinese Theater in Hollywood was staging a prologue to Eddie Cantor's film *Roman Scandals*, which was a musical farce about a young man dreaming that he's back in ancient Rome.

I took a chance. I wired the theatre owner, the

legendary impresario Sid Grauman, that the world's greatest mouth organist (yours truly, of course) was starring at the Chicago Theater, and would be perfect for the warm-up. I signed the telegram 'Louis Lipstone'. Mr Lipstone was the general manager of a huge chain of theatres, roughly speaking the 1930s answer to Bernard Delfont.

I woke up next morning in a cold sweat. I had forged a telegram. I could go to gaol. I raced round to the head office of the Lipstone chain, and pleaded with the receptionist to see 'L.L.' himself. No, I didn't have an appointment. But it was urgent, very urgent. Indeed, virtually a matter of life and death.

I sat in the lobby for an hour. Finally she nodded at me: 'Go on in.'

In his plush office Mr Lipstone sat behind a desk as big as the *Queen Mary*, puffing on a cigar like a torpedo. He kept it in his mouth as he inquired: 'Make it snappy, kid, I'm busy. What's on your mind?'

I started stammering: 'Er, well, it's this way Mr Lipstone, I – ' Then the phone rang. Mr Lipstone raised a hand to silence me, and took the call.

'What? West Coast? Grauman . . . Put him on!'

I looked around for an escape route, but even the windows were closed. Mr Lipstone put his hand over the mouthpiece.

'What's your name? Adler? Grauman says I sent him a wire about you. I never sent no goddamn wire –'

'No sir,' I said, bleating like a sheep caught in a mesh fence. 'I sent it.' I paused, then: 'And I signed your name.'

Louis Lipstone looked at me for a moment that hung like eternity itself. Finally he turned back to the phone.

'Yeah,' he said. 'Sure thing, Sid. The kid's great!'

He put the phone down, folded his hands over his stomach, and regarded me with something like admiration. 'All right, you little sonofabitch. Now prove it!'

At the end of that week, I flew to California.

I didn't have an act, not a real one. I could play numbers, but I had no script or patter to keep the flow going in between the music. At Grauman's I realized I needed something more than nerve to get me through the night.

I checked in to the Roosevelt Hotel, on the other side of the street from Grauman's, and sank my head in my hands while I sought inspiration.

In the end one piece of music swam out to me – Ravel's great 'Bolero', which I had recently played at the Blackhawk nightclub in Chicago, using a dance arrangement by composer Hal Kemp. Unfortunately he had turned Ravel's mighty opus into a foxtrot – and I was stuck with it, as it was the only version I knew.

Disaster loomed. I could hear myself being booed off the stage. I stood in the wings, literally trembling, as a family of acrobats called the Piccianni Troupe somersaulted around the stage, and a female impersonator named Nell Kelly came on as Garbo, proclaiming that she wanted to be alone. I knew how she felt, and wished I could join her.

Too late. I walked out, started off the 'Bolero' –

and for the first forty bars it was fine. I kept in time with the orchestra – but suddenly things started going wrong. They were behind me, or maybe I was behind them. In panic, I waved one arm wildly at them, while keeping the mouth organ to my lips with the other. The orchestra responded. I played with even more fervour, a man possessed, ending with a flourish and a swoop up the notes that even Ravel would never have intended for that final marvellous climactic discord.

I couldn't believe what happened next. The place erupted in a typhoon of cheers, shouts, applause – it stopped the show, and I took no fewer than ten curtain calls. As I came off, sweating in disbelief, the stage manager shouted above the uproar: 'Grauman says: play it again!'

I couldn't. I was exhausted. Perhaps it was instinct, or maybe because I was drained, but I followed the old showbiz maxim and sensibly quit while I was ahead.

Next day the *Variety* and LA *Times* reviews for Eddie Cantor and *Roman Scandals* were all about the kid who stole the show. Phone calls blocked the line to my room at the Roosevelt. The agency was full of plaudits, triumphantly informing me that offers were coming in already.

OK, I thought, get it right this time. I practised all day, listened to a classical recording of the 'Bolero' which I should have done before, got it all into my head. That night I played all the right notes in the right time, relaxing as the orchestra and I performed perfectly at one with each other.

And I flopped! Two modest curtain calls sent me scurrying back to my dressing-room in disbelief. Why?

Sid Grauman provided the answer. He stormed in. 'What the hell's happened to you, kid? You lost your showmanship!'

'What – ?' I began.

He put me right. Showmanship meant flailing my arms around like a banshee, acting as conductor to the band as well as harmonica soloist – in other words, taking over the whole show.

I did my best to explain what had happened. Now I knew what to do, I had the material right, I didn't need the histrionics any more.

'Screw the material,' growled Mr Grauman, putting Ravel firmly in his place. 'Put back the showmanship, OK?'

Well . . . OK. The bandleader didn't talk to me, the orchestra didn't like it, the other performers weren't happy – but the audience loved it.

I chopped down invisible trees for night after night, and the word got round. A new breeze had blown into town.

That was when the William Morris agency decided it was time I started making movies.

I refused to be discouraged by the failure of *Operator 13* to get me in front of the cameras and make me an international movie star. Sure enough, along came *Many Happy Returns*, a comedy about a scatty girl who jinxes her father's department store. George Burns and Gracie Allen were the stars, with Ray Milland as the romantic lead, and the film was pepped up by vaudeville acts that they somehow managed to write into the script.

Burns and Allen, of course, were a delight. As for me, I got to play 'Sophisticated Lady' with the Duke Ellington band, set in a broadcasting studio. My fee was $300. I wouldn't win any Oscars for my facial expressions, but the music sounded great!

It was Duke who introduced me to another legend – Billie Holiday, no less. I was still doing live shows whenever I could, and I found myself in Chicago appearing at the Palmer House. Afterwards Ellington dropped by the dressing-room, and invited me to go on with him to the Grand Terrace on the South Side, a club that was famous for having the best black acts in the country. Earl Hines ran the show, and when we turned up unannounced he asked if we'd play a duet.

'Sure,' said the Duke. 'Why not?' I echoed. We gave them a couple of numbers, and as Duke got up from the piano he said: 'I want you to meet somebody.'

He took me over to a table where a lady was sitting alone. 'Larry,' said Duke, 'meet Billie Holiday.'

I put out a hand: 'How do you do?'

'Man,' said Miss Holiday, in that voice that no one can imitate however hard they try, 'you don't play that fuckin' thing, you *sing* it!'

I've always thought that would make a good epitaph.

* * *

The Maestro in action. An early picture of sartorial elegance.

Top: With Earl Mountbatten at the Albert Hall for a reunion of Burma veterans. In the end he mimed it – but nobody knew.

Above: Teaching one of the showgirls to wing it in an early tour.

Top: There is nothing like a dame – especially if she's Dame Barbara Cartland, on the arms of Mountbatten and Larry.

Above: Time for a waltz: Viennese Night at the Albert Hall in the seventies.

With Melvyn Bragg, whose *South Bank Show* made a special programme of my tribute to George Gershwin.

Eileen Walser, a lovely young model who became the first Mrs Larry Adler.

Top: Mobbed by the troops: a wartime tour with Jack Benny, Martha Tilton – and, on my left, Ingrid Bergman.

Above left: Larry of Arabia.

Above right: Jack Benny and his violin do their best to obliterate the real star of the show. Note the natty suit.

Eileen Walser, a lovely young model who became the first Mrs Larry Adler.

Top: Mobbed by the troops: a wartime tour with Jack Benny, Martha Tilton – and, on my left, Ingrid Bergman.

Above left: Larry of Arabia.

Above right: Jack Benny and his violin do their best to obliterate the real star of the show. Note the natty suit.

Lauren Bacall and Humphrey Bogart in *To Have and Have Not*, the movie in which they first appeared together. It was Bogey who called me a "pain in the ass." From him, that was a compliment!

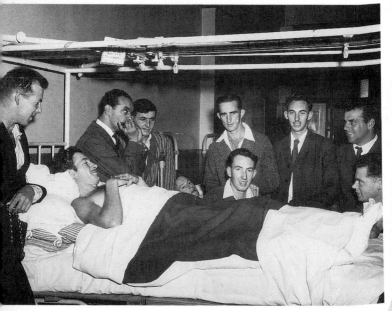

Top: Still in my teens, but I wouldn't miss a chance for a spot of rhythm.

Above: Playing to our boys in a front line hospital in Korea.

I found I got on very well with both the stars and the studio top brass. I was sociable, maybe a little star-stuck but seldom overawed, and just happy to be part of the Hollywood scene. I would grab any chance to mingle with the big names, so when Walter Wanger invited me to his house for dinner, I didn't think twice before accepting.

For some reason the producer had taken a shine to me, and wanted to give my career a little push in the right direction. Maybe it was the twenty weeks I'd had in virtual purdah on *Operator 13*. But since he'd been fired, too, I guess we also had something in common. 'The big boys from MGM are going to be there,' he confided. 'And some other names you'll know. It won't do you any harm at all. And I'll make sure they remember you.'

Despite that last hiccup, Mr Wanger had an impressive track record. He had served with Army Intelligence in World War I, and had actually been on President Woodrow Wilson's staff at the Paris Peace Conference that led to the President getting the Nobel Prize in 1919. After the war he turned to movies, and made his name as a producer with films like *Queen Christina*, with Greta Garbo, and the classic John Ford Western, *Stagecoach*. He became Production Chief of three studios – Paramount, Columbia and MGM. All in all, a good man to have in your corner.

'Larry, I want to spring a little surprise on these people,' Mr Wanger said, beaming at me like a schoolboy who has just hit on a particularly good jape. 'I'll hide you behind the curtain in the dining-room. Stay out of sight. When I give the signal, you start playing!

'They'll wonder where in hell that music's coming from, and when I draw the drapes and they see it's a mouth organ they'll fall flat on their asses with amazement. What d'you say?'

'I say OK,' I told him. I liked it.

Dinner was at seven. People tend to eat early in Hollywood, especially if they've got to be up at dawn next day. Half an hour beforehand I took up my position behind the heavy burgundy-coloured curtains. I could hear voices and laughter from the next room where they were having pre-dinner cocktails.

Mr Wanger had been kind enough to provide me with a chair, but nothing else. Not even a drink. It was an oversight I could live with when I peeped through the curtains and saw the 100-carat guests filing in to take their places around the long dining-table.

Louis B. Mayer, boss of MGM and responsible for its last initial, as well as for its proud slogan: 'More Stars than there are in Heaven'. Irving Thalberg, another MGM czar and supervisor of all their productions, followed Mayer in, a slightly-built man with his lovely actress wife Norma Shearer on his arm. Two other top MGM executives: Eddie Mannix and Benny Thau. And for added glamour: Jeanette MacDonald – 'America's Sweetheart', who else, and the recipient of the legendary, and now laughable 'Indian Love Call' from her long-time screen partner Nelson Eddy. Plus the Orsatti brothers, two of the top agents in Los Angeles.

My heart did a couple of somersaults as I saw my upcoming audience. Wanger ushered them to their seats, and took his own at the head of the table. He was in jovial, expansive mood as he summoned the butler to pour the wine and a waitress to serve the food. Freshly grilled lobster and succulent steak passed in front of my nose, only on the other side of the curtain, and animated chatter filled the room.

My stomach started sending its own love calls out for sustenance, but nobody heard or answered.

I kept my eye fixed on Mr Wanger, peering through the slit in the drapes, waiting for the signal. But not a sign from him, not a peep from me. One hour passed, then another. I stayed still and silent behind the curtain while darkness descended outside.

Finally, coffee was served. My eye went to the slit again – and at last, the signal! Mr Wanger took his handkerchief from his breast pocket, and waved it at me.

I started playing. First, a blues that filled the room with haunting, hypnotic sound, then a jazz classic from Gershwin. Wanger dramatically pulled a cord, and the drapes parted to reveal me standing with one foot on the chair, playing my heart out.

And nobody took a blind bit of notice! Not a single head turned my way. The conversation, if anything, grew more animated. No one bothered to find out where the music came from, or looked at the artiste blowing fit to bust by the window.

Mr Wanger gave me a shrug, and a look that said:
'Sorry kid. I guess I blew it.' Well, that made two
of us.

I walked round the table, out of the room and out
of the house. Nobody even noticed me.

So I went home.

Some years later, in the early 1950s, Mr Wanger
was convicted of shooting and injuring the agent of
his second wife, the actress Joan Bennett, in a
jealous rage because he believed they were having
an affair. He served a brief time in the slammer,
after which he went back to her. They were
divorced in 1962, and Walter died six years later.

So perhaps it was just as well I didn't stay around
to argue that night.

A month after my triumphant session at
Grauman's the MGM publicity office asked me to
escort a starlet back there for one of those hands-in-
the-concrete ceremonies. It can be feet, too, of
course, and I was always struck by how tiny Fred
Astaire's shoes were, there on the sidewalk alongside the hands of Judy Garland and the somewhat
larger breasts of Mae West.

I was happy to oblige, and duly picked up the
starlet at the studio in a stretch limousine, and
whisked her off downtown to the theatre. We
joined a queue of other limos, and while we were
sitting in the log-jam a bunch of kids raced up
waving autograph books. One stuck his head in the
window, looked long and hard at me, then turned
and yelled to the others: 'It's nobody!'

That's how to make an aspiring star feel good.

While on the subject of Grauman's, for some reason they have omitted to ask me to cement a friendship in the pavement, not even with my vital parts if hands are too boring. I would have thought a mouth-imprint would have been a novelty, at least. But I'm still open to invitation.

I was nineteen when I discovered that I was possessed of psychic powers. Frankly, I have always been something of a sceptic when it comes to 'The Twilight Zone', and things that go bump in the night.

But how could I deny this one?

One rainy Saturday afternoon in Palm Springs I found myself with a group of showbiz pals in a villa belonging to Bryan Foy, a son of the famous vaudeville entertainer Eddie Foy. That made him one of the Seven Little Foys – maybe you remember the 1955 Bob Hope biopic of that title? If not, no matter. It wasn't that brilliant.

But Bryan was great fun. In the pecking order he was the Third Little Foy. But he quit the vaudeville circuit to direct comedy shorts at Twentieth Century-Fox, and later wrote for Buster Keaton and other comics.

Rain outside the windows. Cards, booze and gossip inside the comfortable living-room where Bryan was playing host to the music-hall team of Bert Wheeler and Robert Woolsey, together with an assorted crowd of hangers-on.

Somehow the conversation veered round to the

occult, to ghosts, fortune-tellers, and psychic
phenomena. Foy said to me: 'Hey, Adler, did
anyone ever tell you that you were psychic?'

No one ever had. But I had tried my hand at a
few childish experiments in hypnotism, like a lot of
other kids I knew.

'There you go,' said Foy, who seemed to know
what he was talking about. 'What'd I tell you?' He
looked around at the expectant group. 'Hey, I got
an idea. Let's get Larry to pick a winner in the first
race at Hialeah. Can you do it, kid?'

He waved a race card in my face.

'Listen, Bryan, I don't know anything about
horse racing – '

But he wouldn't listen. 'You don't *have* to know
anything. Just look at the names and say the first
one that comes to your mind!'

The whole room was watching me expectantly.

'Well . . . OK. This is silly – but, try Calaveras.'

To my horror, Foy went round with the hat.
People threw dollar notes in, and suddenly we had
a $100 bet. Bryan dialled a number, spoke to his
bookie – and put the whole lot on Calaveras . . .
to win.

The others started pouring out the Scotch. I
stayed on coffee. A poker game began in the far
corner of the room. Then the phone rang.

Foy picked it up. 'Yeah . . . yeah . . . hey! No
kidding! By three lengths, huh? OK, I'll call you
back.'

He turned to me. 'How do you like that! Your
hunch paid off, kid. Eight-to-one shot, we're ahead

eight Cs, and we're cutting you in for ten per cent.
OK, now give us something in the second race.'

I tried to tell them that it was just coincidence,
but my feeble protestations were waved down. 'I
can't do it again, really – '

'Sure you can. Try!'

I stared at the card. A name swam out. 'Bay
Rum,' I said.

The Third Little Foy shook his head. 'Aah, that's
no good. Bay Rum's the odds-on favourite. Pick
another one.'

'No,' I said, with a firmness that surprised
myself. 'Bay Rum is my hunch. That's the name I
see – Bay Rum.'

Reluctantly Foy called his bookie, and put eight
hundred dollars on Bay Rum, to win. Which it
proceeded to do, giving us a pot of $1,200.

It went on like that all afternoon. I just couldn't
lose. By the end of the afternoon the stake was
$20,000.

Foy was ecstatic. 'I knew you'd got it, kid,' he
said, tapping the side of his forehead significantly.
'I can tell these things.' He became businesslike.
'Right, last race. Last time around, and we're all in
clover – hey, baby?'

He thrust the card at me. The rest of the room
had gone suddenly quiet as I ran my eye down it. I
was thinking: *Twenty grand!*

But this time I couldn't see it. 'Bryan,' I said in
despair. 'I don't get any hunch on this one – '

A frown creased the Third Little Foy's normally
amiable brow. 'Sure you do, kid. C'mon, don't let

us down now. You've gotta come up with something. *Concentrate!'*

I stared hard at the list of runners. At last I said:
'I'm sorry. I get two names – '

'Two names is no good, lover boy. Pick one of
them.'

'Bryan, you've got twenty grand riding on this.
What if I pick the wrong one?' I could almost hear
the sound of knuckles cracking around the room.

Foy laughed harshly. 'You haven't picked one
stinker the whole day. C'mon, kiddo – one name,
just one . . . '

'I keep seeing two – ' I shut my eyes, tried
to focus on the card. Then: 'Donatella and No
Cigar . . . '

'And . . . ? Which is it, for Christ's sake – ?'

I took a deep breath. 'No Cigar!'

Foy called the bookie. Twenty grand was too
much to handle, said the voice on the phone. He'd
have to spread it around, play the field. It would
take a little time.

Bryan was expansive. Take all the time you like,
he responded. Just make sure it all goes on No
Cigar, on the nose, to win.

I felt the panic rising. I could have made $2,000
out of it. Why couldn't he just quit?

The phone rang.

Foy picked it up, and I watched his face change
as he heard the news. 'Yeah . . . yeah . . . came
second, huh? Who won? No shit – Donatella, eh?
Well, you can't win 'em all.'

He hung up, and in what can only be termed a

pregnant silence, looked across at me. 'Don't feel bad, kid. It wasn't your fault. Well, not really . . . '

I actually thought I might throw up on the carpet. Twenty grand . . .

Six years go by. Here I am in Romanoff's in 1939, sitting with Charles Laughton and Elsa Lanchester (aka Mrs Charles Laughton), and there across the room in another private booth is Bryan Foy. He's with a group of friends, and he's looking my way, and pointing at me, and laughing as if he's going to fall out of his seat.

And then it hits me.

The whole thing was a set-up. Foy hadn't placed a single bet, and neither had his friends. No money won or lost. Just me, shutting my eyes and visualizing some stupid horse, and believing every second of it.

Foy had simply phoned a friend who had been in on the gag, and played me for a sucker. I went over to him, and shook his hand. 'Six years,' I said. 'And all this time I believed it.'

Wasn't that a beauty?

5

On the Road

*'Thank you very much, Larry. I enjoyed it.
But I think I'll stay being a lesbian.'*

Las Vegas showgirl, in bed

I grew up early and I grew up fast. As a teenager
mixing with gangsters and their molls, as well as
being part of the show-business and jazz scene, I
saw it all.

New Orleans, where I nearly lost my virginity,
turned out to be an eye-popper of a place for a kid
who was still only fourteen years old. On the last
night of our tour there, our cast got together with
the acts from a show called *Radio Romance* at a neigh-
bouring theatre to hire a 'sex circus'.

They took over a basement club, and as I was not
yet fifteen and legally under-age, I was allowed in
without paying. Freebie! The cast were all black.
We sat at tables in the smoke-hazy cellar, and I can
still see those statuesque black showgirls – maybe
hooker is a more accurate term – strolling around
casually picking up dollar bills from the tables with
what is known politely as their genital area! For an

encore they also smoked cigarettes from the same place – and smoke would actually puff out. Don't ask me how.

There was straight screwing on the small stage. Lesbian sex. Gay sex – the man playing the passive role wore a grass skirt, which added an exotic flavour to the proceedings. The climax, if that's the right word, was a donkey and a woman. She lay on her back on a table, and the animal was guided to mount and enter her.

You'd think it would be enough to put me off sex for life. But curiously, all this flaunted eroticism roused my youthful male ardour, though that night I certainly wasn't going to touch any of the goods on sale.

We flew on to Toledo, where my tap dancing chum Peter made up a foursome with two very attractive young ladies fresh out of high school. He rented a car, and we took them out for dinner.

At the end of the meal I felt a nudge on my knee. Peter was prodding me under the table with a box of chocolates he had produced from nowhere. He gave me a wink. 'Pass these around, Larry.'

For some reason I was suspicious. Why that leer? I kept the chocolates hidden.

We took the girls home, and found that all we got was a goodnight kiss. Peter was mad as hell. In the car on the way back to our hotel he shouted: 'You goddamn fool! I spent twenty-five bucks on that stuff!'

'What!' I said. 'On chocolates – ?'

'No, you dumb idiot. For Spanish Fly!'

Now that old myth about Spanish Fly being an aphrodisiac has long been exploded. But in those days I believed it. And what I did know was that it was a drug, and a dangerous one. We could have been gaoled for years. I hid the chocolate box in a drawer in my hotel room.

The following week we had moved on to Cleveland. Peter came into the dressing-room. 'Got the chocolates?' he asked.

My God! The chocolates! They were still in the drawer back in the hotel in Toledo. I remembered that the acts on the circuit following us featured someone I knew, a Chinese tenor named Jue Fong. I tracked him down, and asked him if he could get those chocolates out of the hotel. 'Don't eat 'em,' I warned. 'I'll tell you why when I see you. Just destroy them!'

'OK, Larry,' said Fong – no, he did *not* say Rally. He rang back an hour later. 'I got in – but nothing there,' he said.

'Well, thanks anyway.' I waited to hear about a Toledo chambermaid leaping on six bellboys, but thankfully – nothing. I just hope somebody enjoyed them.

At fifteen, I achieved my first mention in the gossip columns. Now? I've had so many I could paper the walls of my flat with them, and probably the whole block too. But what a thrill it was to see my name in print for the first time – and in the New York *Daily News*, no less.

Sidney Skolsky, the popular columnist for that illustrious paper, had taken a shine to me after seeing the show, and remarked in his column on my resemblance to Eddie Cantor. Oddly enough, Cantor too had begun his professional career at the age of fourteen, starting out as a singing waiter on Coney Island. They called him 'banjo eyes', which I suppose wasn't particularly flattering – nor to me, now I think of it – but he sure stood out in a crowd.

Eddie turned up at the Palace Theater the next night to see my act. And, I suspect, to check for possible libel! Afterwards he came backstage.

'Yes, kid, you sure do look like me. Would you like to come on my next tour?' he asked.

Would I! Eddie Cantor was a b-i-g star, and the timing was perfect as my own season was coming to an end. The agency was delighted, too.

We started out at the Mastbaum Theater in Philadelphia, a massive auditorium which at that time was the biggest in the whole of America. Would the sounds from my harmonica fill it? No chance to find out. All I had was two lines in a walk-on gag.

Cantor had five daughters. He made jokes about them, and that's why he wanted me in his act. I came bounding on the stage wearing a Western Union uniform and pillbox hat, and handed him a telegram.

He took it, looked at me, did a double-take, and said to the audience: 'Hey, this kid looks like me. How old are you, son?'

'I'm fifteen, sir.'

Cantor would count on his fingers, muttering to himself. Then: 'Where are you from, son?'

'I'm from Baltimore, sir.'

More counting, more murmuring. Then a sigh of relief. 'No, I was in Seattle.'

For that one lousy joke Eddie Cantor paid me $125 a week – and that was *money*! I didn't get to play the mouth organ, but at least I got to pay the rent.

My final date with the Cantor show was a week at the RKO Theater in Brooklyn. On the same bill was a kids' revue produced by another friend in the business, Gus Edwards.

I had to be a big shot. I bragged to some of the kids that I was getting $500 a week. They believed me – and put in a formal complaint to Gus. How come *they* weren't getting five big ones a week?

Gus told Cantor. And I was fired.

To this day I regret my own stupidity. Eddie Cantor had treated me with great generosity, and I could have learned a lot if I'd stayed in his camp. In the years that followed I would play backing music to some of his records. But he never asked me to appear with him again.

Fred Astaire and I were locked into rivalry. Not over a dame, though I loved his sister Adele dearly, and was constantly telling her so. But over the piano. Each of us was convinced he was the better player.

On tour with the show *Smiles*, where the Astaires did their famous run-around act, jogging round the stage in rhythm, we would race to get to the rehearsal room first and grab the piano stool. On stage I did a duet with Fred called 'Young Man of Manhattan', which ended when he used his equally famous cane as a machine-gun, mowing down the other dancers, and finally me. I would expire on stage with a suitable groan from my harmonica, and lie there while the applause swamped us. It was a brilliant number.

You can imagine my delight when Adele asked *me* – not her brother – to accompany her on the piano on a radio chat show hosted by Alexander Woollcott, the drama critic of the *New Yorker* magazine. After the interview Adele would sing 'If You Would Always be Good to Me', from our show.

'Sorry, Fred,' I said smugly as we left for the studio. 'I think this clinches it. Perhaps you'll let me get to the piano first from now on.'

Fred ground his teeth, but couldn't do much about it.

But at the studio: disaster! When we ran through the number for sound balance, Adele said: 'I can't sing that key. It's too low. Put it up half a tone.'

Easy enough? Not for me. I played the piano by ear, the same way I play the mouth organ, and my only key was C. Putting it up half a tone meant it would be C sharp, almost entirely on the black notes, and I knew I couldn't handle it.

I tried explaining this to Adele, who responded briskly: 'Nonsense. You can play anything.'

Well, thanks for the compliment – but even the composer, Vincent Youmans, wouldn't have recognized the sounds that emanated from the piano that evening. It went out live, Adele squawked her way through it, and finally ran from the studio in tears. Woollcott didn't even say thank you to me. In fact, he ignored me altogether.

As for Fred, he had a smirk on his face that lasted the rest of the tour. Next day I walked into my dressing-room to find a newspaper lying on the table under the mirror. The *Herald-Tribune*. Only Fred had manufactured a headline right across the front page.

In two-inch capitals it shouted at me: LARRY ADLER IS A SHIT!

As for the lovely Adele, for some reason she didn't seem keen on my ever playing for her again.

Fred Astaire had one direct influence on me. He never wore a belt, always a tie round his waist. Why? I asked him once, and he replied simply: 'Because I like it.' I borrowed the habit from him, and for the past sixty years I have always worn a tie to keep up my trousers.

Weird? What was good enough for Fred Astaire is good enough for me. He was my sartorial hero. When I first came to England I went straight to his tailors, Kilgour, French and Stanbury in Savile Row, and ordered a set of tails in vicuna cloth, just like Astaire.

One of the most incredible events I ever witnessed took place in the Waldorf-Astoria ballroom in 1932. Imagine, if you will, a stage with two *dozen* black concert grand pianos ranged in a horseshoe around one other concert grand.

It was a black-tie event to raise funds for charity, and the cream of New York high society had fought for tickets. When I took my seat, I saw why.

The curtain went up, and on to that stage walked the greatest composers of the day, two by two, all in white tie and tails. George Gershwin, Jerome Kern, Noel Coward, Sigmund Romberg, Irving Berlin, Hoagy Carmichael, Harold Arlen, Sammy Fain, Johnny Green, Arthur Schwartz, Burton Lane, Harry Revel, Richard Rodgers, Duke Ellington, Benny Davis, Fats Waller . . . how's that for starters?

They sat down, two to each piano, while one went to the central concert grand and played his best-known melody, solo. On the second chorus all the other composers at their pianos would join in. I've never seen anything like it before or since, and I don't think a spectacle like that can ever be staged again. It still sends shivers down my spine when I think of it.

I had been invited along by Gus Edwards, the producer who had unwittingly caused me to be fired by Eddie Cantor. No hard feelings. He was a good friend, in fact, and felt I was destined for great things. Which is why, after the show was over, he took me backstage, threw open the door of the main dressing-room, and announced loudly: 'Quiet, please! Gentlemen, will you kindly listen to this young man!' He turned to me. 'Go ahead, kid. Play!'

The room fell into a deathly hush. I looked

around at the faces that turned to me, and felt my knees go wobbly. Well, wouldn't you?

Kern . . . Gershwin . . . Coward . . . Rodgers . . . Berlin . . . they were all there, relaxing after the great night. And along comes little old me to play them a tune on my mouth organ!

But I did it. In that silence, I fished into my pocket, pulled out my tried and trusted friend, and gave them my best shot with 'Smoke Gets in Your Eyes', with its composer, Mr Jerome Kern, staring me in the face from ten feet away.

When you've been through that, I tell you, nothing's going to faze you again! At the end, the greatest living men in music – OK, there were others, but these would do for now – put their hands together and applauded me the way they themselves had been applauded fifteen minutes earlier.

It was a moment to treasure. And it led to good things. Noel Coward offered me a part in a revue he was putting on in London, which in the end I was unable to take as I was on the road elsewhere. But we would keep in touch. I was with him at a party years later when someone said to him: 'I am invariably kind to my inferiors.' Coward replied: 'How clever of you to find them.'

In London I was having dinner at the Ivy restaurant when Noel walked in alone. He spotted me, and came over. 'Dear boy,' he said, in those inimitable cut-glass accents, 'I have had the most *horrendous* evening.' He sat down at the table. It seemed he had been at the opening night of the stage version of *Gone with the Wind*, with Bonnie Langford – at that time a child wonder of the age and stage – and hated every minute of it. Especially Bonnie's performance, including what she sang and the way she sang it.

Apparently a horse had also obeyed a call of nature on the stage. 'Do you realize, Larry,' said Coward, 'that if they had only had the foresight to stuff the child up the horse's arse they could have averted *two* catastrophes.'

Arthur Schwartz invited me to join his show. Others made encouraging noises. I shook hands all round, and knew I would see these icons of the music and jazz scene again. All in all, I'd call that night at the Waldorf-Astoria one to remember.

Strange things happen when you're on the road. For one thing, you never quite know where you're going to end up – or with whom! In Chicago in a bar after the show one night I met a woman who insisted I took her back to my hotel room and made love to her – but not straight sex, oh no. Anything but that.

We threshed around in every position you'll find in the *Kama Sutra* except the missionary. When I asked why we couldn't just make love in the time-honoured ordinary way, she looked quite shocked. 'Oh no. That would mean I'm being unfaithful to my husband!' she said. Well, you work it out.

And in Las Vegas I made a pass at a beautiful showgirl one time in the 1950s when I was playing at El Rancho Vegas. Her name was Anita, she was tall, blonde, and had the kind of legs – as they once said of Shirley Maclaine – that start at the shoulders.

I bought her a drink, and launched into my verbal foreplay – of which I have to say I'm rather proud. She interrupted me. 'Larry, before you go any further, I think you ought to know that I'm a lesbian.'

'Oh,' I said. My witty conversation dried up. We finished our drinks, shook hands solemnly, and that was that. Until three days later. Out of the blue, up hove Anita. 'I've been thinking, Larry,' she said. 'You seem like a nice fellow. I've never had a hetero-sexual experience. Shall we – ?' Her own words, exactly.

Nothing loth, I took her upstairs to my suite, and we made long, lingering love on the king-size bed. When it was over, and I lay back on the sheets, pleasantly exhausted, she turned on one elbow,

'Thank you very much, Larry,' she said. 'I enjoyed it. But I think I'll stay being a lesbian.'

I suppose ego and stardom walk in each other's shadow. I've seen enough of both, in all sorts of people, places and situations. Some are bearable, others are intolerable.

I have to say that I have never liked Mr Frank Sinatra (in deference to his wishes, because he wants it that way, I always call him Mister). I don't like what he does to songs. We have met a few times, usually at parties or receptions, and he has always been perfectly courteous, calls me Larry, and nods back when I call him Mr Sinatra.

I still don't like him.

Mr Sinatra is a one-man power-base, but even he can get his come-uppance. One time in the late 1940s I was at a Beverly Hills party in North Linden Drive thrown by Henry Ginsberg, the head of Paramount. Frank – er, Mr Sinatra – was there, along with a roll call of celebrity names.

There was a stir in the room, the crowd parted – and I found myself shaking hands with Cole Porter, who had been pushed in sitting in a wheelchair. 'A horse fell on me,' he explained, when I asked what had happened. 'Crushed my legs.' In fact – poor guy – he had to endure numerous operations and in 1958 had a leg amputated.

But he always remained cheerful, though he could be acerbic if the occasion required it. Mr Sinatra saw him, had a few words, then beckoned to his accompanist Jimmy Van Heusen who was in the far corner of the room. 'I want to sing Cole Porter *to* Cole Porter,' he announced grandly.

We gathered round the piano. Mr Sinatra started to warble the strains of 'I Get a Kick Out of You'. On the second chorus, for no apparent reason, he sang: 'I get a boot out of you – '

Cole Porter's face darkened in rage. 'Get me out of here!' he said, before the song was even finished. Someone pushed the wheelchair to the door, and Porter was gone. Later he sent Mr Sinatra a wire. It read: 'If you don't like my songs the way I write them, why sing them?' Ouch!

Same with Danny Kaye. I didn't care too much
for him, either, though you can't deny the man had
enormous talent. He was about to open in the
Broadway show that would make his name – *Lady
in the Dark*, a spectacular musical about a fashion
magazine editor (female) who has man trouble,
boosted by the slogan: 'The minx in mink with a yen
for men!' Ginger Rogers would later star in the 1944
screen version.

Danny and I had the same agents at that time:
William Morris. We would meet in the offices and
exchange a few words, and bump into one another
on the party circuit.

One such occasion was at the home of a Hollywood producer who rejoiced in the name of Arthur
Hornblow Junior. Believe it or not, he had been a
counter-espionage agent for the US Government
before turning to make movies with titles like *The
Heavenly Body*, with Hedy Lamarr, and *Desire Me*,
with Greer Garson. Mr Hornblow's own heavenly
body at that time was his wife Myrna Loy, who had
arranged his fortieth birthday party at their
sumptuous mansion.

It was Arthur's party – but what happened? In
the middle of the jollities, Danny Kaye suddenly
climbed on to the table in the middle of the room,
called for silence, and went into one of his numbers.
He raved around like a lunatic, a mixture of mono-
logue and song that seemed to go on for ever.

It ruined the party. To complete the embarrassment, at the end there was no applause at all, just
a stony silence before we all started talking again.

6

Bolero

'Larry, you like jokes. Now let me tell you what makes a great comedian.'

Charlie Chaplin

Let's get serious for a moment – but not for too long. I had made Ravel's marvellous 'Bolero' virtually my own – long before Dudley Moore and Bo Derek brought it fresh notoriety in the film *10*, and given it a huge hype as obligatory background music to love-making.

I just wonder what Maurice Ravel would have made of it. I was in Paris, and the 'Bolero' was the big climax to my act at the Alhambra, when I had a call from an old friend, Jacques Lyon, who ran a record shop on the Champs-Elysées. Ravel, the composer himself, had learned that I was playing his great work, and wanted to hear it, from my own lips, so to speak.

I blinked at that one. I had always been understandably hesitant to play any work in front of the person who had composed it, but the idea of playing the 'Bolero' in front of Ravel brought me out in a cold sweat. But . . . it was a rare chance to meet a historic figure, and I couldn't let it slip. I put my harmonica in my pocket – but as a precaution I took the 78 record I had made the previous year along as well. If he wanted me to play, I'd need the accompaniment. As it turned out, the mouth organ stayed in my pocket.

Jacques drove us out to Montfort-L'Amaury, a suburb a few miles outside the centre of Paris, and located the house. Ravel opened the door himself, a dignified man in his sixties with a presence about him that you could almost touch. After perfunctory greetings and some animated conversation in French with my escort, he took the record out of its sleeve and placed it on the turntable.

It had been a big seller, that record, and I was proud of it. But sitting in his front room, with only the light from a table lamp playing on the maestro's features as he sat intently listening to my intepretation of his work, I felt the imperfections stood out like warts.

It was only the one side of a 78, but it seemed to drag on for ever. Ravel sat motionless, his great head bowed. When it reached its final crashing cacophony, he broke the silence, directing his words at Jacques.

My friend said: 'The master he say you play it very fast. Why?'

Oh! I had no idea why. I had no idea that I *did* play it fast. Ravel spoke again.

'The master he says you have made cuts, you do not play the whole piece. Why?'

I explained that in the music halls where I performed, my act ran to fifteen minutes – the length of 'Bolero'. I had to play something else as well. No criticism, but to include it I had to make cuts.

Jacques passed on the information. Ravel frowned. Jacques again: 'The master he ask: do you know Arturo Toscanini?'

Yes, I nodded. I had met him.

'The master he say that Toscanini plays the whole thing.'

Well, he had me there. The conversation languished. Once more, silence deepened over the room. Out of sheer embarrassment I held the record out for Ravel to sign – the one and only time in my life I have ever asked for an autograph. Ravel looked taken aback.

Jacques said: 'The master say, he thought the record was for him.'

Now it was my turn to be surprised. The master had given every sign of loathing the record, and probably me as well. Then he lifted up his hands, and held them out to me. They were shaking. Through Jacques, he told me that he had the palsy, and had written nothing in five years.

It was hard to find anything more to say. We left with a final few banal words of farewell. A few days later Jacques phoned me. 'Come over at once. The master is here.'

In a room at the rear of the record shop Ravel was huddled in an armchair, muffled in a heavy overcoat and scarf. He explained that, by sitting in a dark room and concentrating, he had been able to steady his hand long enough to write his signature, and he had brought the record back for me.

I was both touched and honoured. How could I tell the great Maurice Ravel that I hadn't really wanted his autograph in the first place.

A year later I was hired to play as a soloist in a series of concerts with the Philadelphia Orchestra. During rehearsals the conductor, Paul Caston, suggested that at some point I should do an encore.

Naturally, I chose 'Bolero', which I was enjoying playing and which had virtually become my party piece.

The librarian in the contracts department objected. Performing fees to the composer or to his estate cost an arm and a leg anyway, and that was for just one rendering. Fees for an encore were not worth it.

'Oh,' I said, defeated. Then I remembered something. The offices of Ravel's publishers Elkan-Vogel were actually in Philadelphia. I took a fast cab, and walked in and announced myself. Mr Elkan emerged from an inner office, greeted me cordially, and told me he knew all about me.

'Our client Mr Ravel has left instructions that you are to have free rights to play the "Bolero" in whatever medium you please,' he said.

I went back to the theatre with the good news. Playing the encore that night gave me an extra buzz – because I knew that right was unique to me, and would last for my own lifetime.

* * *

Only on the rarest occasions have I had problems with conductors, and I have been soloist with the best. Names like Sir Georg Solti, Sir Malcolm Sargent, Sir Adrian Boult . . . and others, without titles but distinguished in their own right, whom music scholars will recognize: Monteux, Ancerl, Johnson, Bakaleinikoff, Gould and Cameron among them.

One of the conductors unbecoming (as far as I was concerned) was Eugene Ormandy. I met him when I was booked as soloist with the Detroit Symphony for a radio hour. He disliked me on sight, scarcely acknowledging me when I was introduced at the studio. As often happens in these cases, the feeling was mutual.

At the rehearsal I was kept waiting in a small ante-room until the last minute, so that I only had time to run through my piece, the Vivaldi Violin Concerto in A Minor, just the once. I was seething when I gave the concert-maestro my key of 'A'.

'What is this "A"?' demanded Ormandy.

I explained with over-elaborate patience, as if talking to a ten-year-old, that the mouth organ is a fixed-reed instrument, that I couldn't tune it, and that the orchestra would have to tune to me.

'What!' thundered Ormandy. 'This is ridiculous!'

The orchestra sat up and paid attention. This was blowing up into something they'd be able to write home about.

'Mr Ormandy,' I said, loud and clear. 'I played *this* work with *this* orchestra last year. If you feel that you cannot conduct for me, we will play it without you.'

Someone in the orchestra behind him snickered. Others gasped audibly. You do not talk that way to the chief conductor of a major symphony orchestra.

There was a long, significant pause. I held his eye, and I held my ground. Finally Ormandy tapped the rostrum with his baton.

'Let us begin the first movement!'

We went through the three movements like a dream, without a single hitch, hiccup or hesitation. Ormandy gave an exemplary performance, and I made sure I did too.

Afterwards he didn't say a word to me. And I could hear the sound of my footsteps on the studio floor as I left.

In 1940 Dinah Shore and I provided the cabaret at an elite dinner given by the White House Correspondents for President Roosevelt.

Now I was a strong Roosevelt man, and this was the famous occasion where he made his 'destroyers for bases' speech which made headlines around the world.

I played my guts out. And I got a standing ovation, which in those days was a rare honour. Today, you get one if you lift the piano lid – though maybe it depends on what you lift it with.

The sea of applause followed me off the stage and into a side room, where I tucked my harmonica away, mopped my brow, and was about to go back to the tables when a lady accosted me.

'Larry,' she said effusively, 'it's *wonderful* to hear you – and in such good form.'

Now I've met a lot of women. I thought to myself: I know her, but from where?

'Thank you very much,' I said. Then, after a slight pause: 'Er – I know your face. But . . . I just can't think of your name – '

'Mrs Roosevelt,' she said, and like the perfect hostess she was, kept her smile intact.

As for me, there are times when you really do wish the floor would open up and swallow you.

The one and only C.B. Cochran, showman *extraordinaire*, brought me to Britain. He caught my act in New York, liked it, and invited me to take a chancen to conquer the other side of the Atlantic.

'There's no contract, no guarantees, and you pay your own expenses,' he said. 'But I tell you this, son. If C.B. Cochran comes back with a mouth organist, it'll make news!'

Heck, I would have paid *him*!

We sailed on the *Aquitania*, and I spent most of the time playing table tennis. The Atlantic was feeling particularly benign. By the time we docked at Southampton, Mr Cochran was calling me Larry. I was still calling him Mr Cochran. His wife and his female stars called him 'Cockie', but I never got that familiar. All I know is that for a man so powerful in show business, I had never known one with such warmth and kindness.

C.B. was right about making news. The press

turned out in force at Southampton to see who this new discovery was, what he looked like, and what he could do. Up to now, the great showman had always come back from America with a glamour girl in tow. Now, here was a little guy with a mouth organ.

They came aboard for an impromptu press conference, where Mr Cochran grandly announced that my harmonica could replace an entire symphony orchestra – and would be doing just that at the Albert Hall, no less!

Next day the papers were full of it. I was on page one, even if the reporter from *The Times* mistakenly called me a trombonist, while C.L. Graves wrote a full-page poem in *Punch* gloomily predicting the end of civilization in Denmark Street, otherwise Tin Pan Alley, as he knew it, and the dissolution of all Britain's major orchestras, made redundant by my mouth organ . . .

But it meant I had arrived!

Cochran put me into his revue *Streamline* at the Palace Theatre, and I closed the first half with 'Bolero', against the setting of a large white screen behind with a projector in the footlights, so that a huge shadow of me was beamed on to the screen. It was very effective, and Cochran's faith in me was justified. The show ran for fifteen weeks.

During that time Cochran and his delightful wife Evelyn took me under their wing, introduced me to London society, and even allowed me to practise on their magnificent Broadwood grand piano at their house in Montagu Square, off Knightsbridge.

Mrs C.B. told me that composers such as George Gershwin, Cole Porter, Richard Rodgers and Noel Coward had all sat on that stool and composed their music on that very piano.

'And do you know, Larry – their spirits seem to linger in the air, and sometimes you can even hear them sigh,' she said, a little wistfully.

One day I was alone in the house playing the piano – when, in the middle of a tune, I heard the distinct sound of someone sighing. The hairs on the back of my neck rose. Christ, the place *was* haunted!

Then I pulled myself together, and the practical side of my nature reasserted itself. Come on, Adler! Something must be causing it. I began tapping each key once to see if anything made that sighing sound. Then I found it – C above middle C. Hit that note, and right away you had a sighing spirit emanating from the bowels of the piano.

I lifted the lid, peered around – no joy. Then I went over the piano inch by inch, and at last found the solution. One leg had a loose metal ring around it – as simple as that. When high C was struck the ring would produce a sympathetic vibration, straight from the grave.

One of the nicest things I can think of to say about myself is that I never told Mrs Cochran.

That Christmas was among the happiest of my life. Evelyn Cochran arrived at the theatre on Christmas Eve with a present for me: a dozen monogrammed handkerchiefs. I had had a silver baton made for the show's conductor, Charles

Prentice. And for C.B. himself, a solid silver cigar cutter in the shape of a mouth organ.

Early in the New Year, after one show, I was with some of the other acts at the exotically-named Shim-Sham Club in Mayfair. A man came up to our table, and told me he wanted to photograph me – and he made it sound that I was the lucky one.

'Come to my studio in the morning,' he said.

Why not? I liked his arrogance, and next day made my way to his studio. It turned out to be merely a small flat in Chelsea. He didn't *have* a studio, just a Leica camera and a few lights. But the photos made a double-page spread in the *Bystander*, one of the fashionable magazines of its day, and it didn't do me any harm at all.

He told me later that they were the first pictures he had ever had published. By the way, his name was Baron.

I was in such demand through all the publicity of my arrival and C.B.'s sterling efforts to make sure the whole country knew of my existence that I found myself playing *four* places in the same evening.

First, the show. Then a sprint out of the stage door at the interval, and into a fast taxi to the Trocadero in Piccadilly. Then another taxi to the Empress Rooms in Knightsbridge. And finally, some time after midnight, the Savoy with Carroll Gibbons's orchestra. I did other dates in cabaret at the Berkeley and the Dorchester, too. Oh yes, I was in the fast lane all right, and loving every minute of it.

In addition, I cut my first record, courtesy of C.B.
Cochran. It was like having a first baby: on the
Columbia label I spent several days in a West End
studio recording 'Smoke Gets in Your Eyes', 'The
Continental', 'Londonderry Air', Kreisler's 'Caprice
Viennois' and Falla's 'Ritual Fire Dance'. And,
naturally, Ravel's 'Bolero'.

They released 'Smoke' and 'The Continental'
together first, and it became the biggest seller of the
year. If they'd had 'Top of the Pops', you'd have
seen me on it, up there at No. 1.

C.B. arranged a charity concert at Queen's
Hall in Mayfair, with household names like
Ronald Frankau and George Robey on the bill. I
found Frankau vulgar and totally unfunny. But I
was charmed by George Robey and his garrulous
humour. For openers, he would begin: 'In the early
days, Mother and Father went up the river for a
lark. I'm the lark.' I suppose, as Frank Carson
would say, it's the way you tell 'em.

I was part of a cabaret act with Max Miller, the
most famous music-hall 'cheekie chappie' of them
all. His innuendos were even more outrageous than
Frankau's smutty double meanings. In his loud
check suit and snazzy white hat, Max was an
original. His machine-gun delivery kept us all in
stitches, both sides of the curtain.

Max told me how he managed to get himself
banned from the London Palladium. He appeared
on a Royal Variety Show, with King George V and
Queen Mary watching from the Royal Box. Max

began a story which everyone swiftly realized was going to be dirty.

It began with a drunken sailor chasing a young boy up a dark alley. Max got deeper into the murky waters, but just at the crucial point of the joke he stopped dead in his verbal tracks, looked up at the Royal Box and its distinctly unamused occupants, and said: 'No, not tonight. Any other night, yes. But *not* tonight!'

I thought that was hilarious, and told him so. His reply: 'Larry, if you don't take risks, you're not an artist.'

It still got him banned, and for several years. Come to think of it, I never did find out the punchline to that story, either.

C.B. kept my name going. He booked me on to 'Henry Hall's Guest Night', one of the most popular family BBC radio shows of all time. Listening figures were into millions. Cochran was to introduce me himself, I would play two numbers with the orchestra: 'Smoke Gets in Your Eyes' and 'Bolero'. Everything was set, we were going out live.

Red light. C.B. gives me a splendid introduction. I play the first haunting number, and get a thumbs-up from the control booth.

Now it's Cochran's turn again, this time to announce 'Bolero'. But – nothing. Just silence. They call it 'dead air'. I look round, and find C.B. desperately searching through his pockets. Somehow he has managed to mislay his glasses, and also managed to forget the second number. My God, it's only one word!

Panic in the studio. The producer is signalling frantically from behind the glass window, beseeching C.B. to forget the glasses, for Chrissakes, and say *something*. Cochran launches into a complete ad-lib, making it up as he goes along just to fill that awful silence.

To my horror I hear him say: 'Well, folks, Larry uses a new mouth organ every time he plays – don't you, Larry?'

Well, no, I didn't. But how could I contradict my friend – and boss – on the air? I say: 'Yes, sure I do, fine, ha-ha, that's right.' Then I play the 'Bolero', and hope everyone will forget.

They didn't. The letters came in by the sackful, thousands of them, all asking for my used mouth organs.

It was the beginning of a legend that never died. But I don't, I don't!

I have always skated on thin ice, and been proud of it. So when I heard that the skating couple of Jayne Torvill and Christopher Dean were going to use my record of 'Summertime' for their backing in the European ice dance championships in 1981, I was thrilled to bits. They are such a delightful pair to watch, bringing a freshness, joy and vivacity to the ice rink that is quite special.

Also, of course, they had made their name with the 'Bolero', which gives us something extra in common. But I couldn't help wondering why they had chosen 'Summertime'. I found the answer in

John Hennessy's book *Torvill and Dean* – now why can't *I* think of titles like that?

Dean told the author: 'We were all quite adamant that our blues routine should be completely different from anything the others might offer. We tried to think of the obvious thing, and go the opposite way. So we came up with the idea of going back to the roots, a sort of sad lament rather than an upbeat sexy blues.

'We had no clear vision of the music at that time. Someone suggested that it ought to be a strong single instrument – something like a harp, I think he had in mind.

'But a few months beforehand I had seen a Michael Parkinson programme on television in which Larry Adler was a guest, and he had played a great harmonica number with a violinist. That memory remained with me, and the next day we went to the Nottingham Library and pulled out a Larry Adler LP.

'The track that most appealed to us both was Gershwin's "Summertime", very striking and evocative. Our main doubt was that it was so well known that somebody else might use it. Choosing a piece of music is fraught with the same difficulty as a woman choosing a hat!

'We experimented with other music and other instruments, but we kept coming back to Larry Adler and "Summertime". Our minds were finally made up by the strong sound the record made over the system at the rink.'

It was true. I had been on Parky's chat show on

BBC-TV with Itzhak Perlman – a 'violinist?' I don't think he'd have liked *that* – with Lilli Palmer as the other guest.

At the rehearsal, Michael asked: 'Would you two play something together?' We were both agreeable. I suggested a movement of the Bach Double Violin Concerto.

Perlman objected. 'We would need the music. It would look too formal.'

Yes, he had a point. We ran through a few other pieces, none of which was quite right. Then I suggested 'Summertime' from *Porgy and Bess*. We had played a few bars, when I raised a hand and stopped it.

'That's the one,' I said. 'But let's not kill it in rehearsal. We both know the tune. Let's just go out and do it.'

Which is what we did. I still think today that it is the single best thing I have ever done on TV. The BBC ran it again on 'The Best of Parkinson', a summary of his TV career, and I'm just glad I was part of it.

Torvill and Dean had already skated their way into the British public's heart with 'Bolero'. Now they did it again. In *The Times* next day, the review stated: 'What Adler did for Gershwin, Torvill and Dean now did for Adler.'

I'm not arguing. It seemed that between us, we had brought summertime to England. And that's a feat in itself.

7

Royal Flush at the Thursday Club

'No one will ever believe me when I tell them I held Larry Adler's organ!'

The Queen Mother

I have never been intimidated by the royal family, and I've met all the 'senior royals'. But then, I'm not in awe of *anybody*. I judge people by accomplishment. I like to think I could never be struck dumb by anybody.

Wait! There was someone – and it happened twice. Same man – total silence. For once – no, twice – the Adler tongue was stilled. But when you're talking about Rachmaninov, I reckon that's excusable. I was introduced to him by Sir Henry Wood at a concert he was giving in Sheffield in 1937, and all I could do was stare up at this tall, distinguished, sombre man – and I couldn't say a word! I was so overawed I didn't even ask him if he'd consider writing a piece for my mouth organ.

Six years later I met him again in Chicago. Similar introduction – same effect. I stayed tongue-tied.

I daren't think what he made of me, and sadly I never had a chance to get third time lucky. Sergei Vasilyevich Rachmaninov, the greatest interpreter of romantic composers, died that same year, 1943, at the age of seventy.

At least my unusual reticence never happened with anybody else. I am always surprised how so many people, from millionaire moguls to top Hollywood stars, get a dose of the shakes when they meet the Queen in a line-up at some royal command performance. Not me. Einstein and Freud, maybe. Royalty, never.

I'm respectful, of course, whenever I meet any of them. But I can't even bring myself to address them by their title – all that fawning 'Your Royal Highness' and the rest of it just isn't for me.

In a line-up, when I'm introduced I simply say: 'How do you do?' They don't seem to mind, although some of the shivering minions around them look a bit pale. But I'm not committing *lèse-majesté* by saying anything like 'Hi, kiddo!' Now that *would* be a ticket to the Tower.

As a result, I find the royals relax in my presence. Particularly the Queen Mother, who is always a laid-back lady anyway. She has a great sense of fun, almost mischievous, and in my book she's undoubtedly the most humorous of all of them.

One time I was invited to play at Clarence House, a pleasant evening in the music room in front of a gathering of her private guests. Afterwards the Queen Mother came up and asked if she could see my harmonica. She took it from me, turned it over and over, peered intently at the holes, and finally handed it back.

'Do you know,' she announced brightly to whoever was within earshot, 'no one will ever believe me when I tell them I held Larry Adler's organ!' There are some moments when one is totally lost for a reply. Well, what would *you* have said?

The truth is that the royal family can be pretty heavy going, and sometimes it gets a bit uphill when you're chatting to them. In 1993 they held various events to celebrate the fortieth anniversary of the Queen's accession.

One of these was a mega-concert at Earl's Court, with the whole royal family in attendance and Raymond Baxter introducing the various items, expounding on the historical milestones that had passed by over the intervening years.

I overheard him at rehearsal intoning: 'In 1968, the first test-tube baby was born.' It gave me an idea.

I caught him on a quiet moment having a cup of coffee, and said: 'Listen Ray, this could give me a good entrance line. Could you say: ". . . And we have that test-tube baby with us tonight – Larry Adler!" What do you think?'

'I like it,' he said, laughing. And duly produced the line, which went down well, too.

Afterwards the royals trooped backstage to meet the artists. Prince Andrew approached me, and in all seriousness asked: 'Were you really a test-tube baby?' Surely I looked older than twenty-five? I was born in 1914, when the only test tubes were the kind they burned litmus paper over, but how could I tell him that?

Hot on Andrew's heels came Prince Charles, who said loudly: 'God, how I used to love you on "The Goon Show".' Which did little to endear him to me – that harmonica player, of course, being Max Geldray. I was never on 'The Goon Show' in my life.

Up came the Queen. 'Do you know,' I said, 'That I played for you when you were ten years old?'

'Oh,' said the monarch. 'What occasion was that?'

I said: 'In Edinburgh. You and your sister sat on the floor, and your mother and father sat behind you.'

There was a long pause while both HM and I thought of something more to say. Finally she broke the silence. 'How kind of you to remember so far back,' she said. And moved on down the line. Yes, it's tough meeting the royals sometimes – for all concerned.

I'm sure Prince Charles is a very nice chap. It's just unfortunate that I have never got along well with the heir to the throne. The other occasions were not exactly moments to treasure all one's life, either.

I was playing in the grounds of Buckingham Palace at a reunion of war veterans. A large marquee had been erected at the back, the sun was shining on a perfect summer's day, and the band of the Grenadier Guards had been playing on the lawn. Now it was my turn.

I stepped on to the small stage as the elderly veterans clustered around. And I gave them – what else but 'Summertime'?

Just as I started, I heard a woman laugh. Out of the corner of my eye I checked the source – and there, less than twenty feet away, was Prince Charles in animated conversation with a lady who obviously found everything he had to say screechingly funny. I rolled both my own banjo eyes at him as I played on, beseeching him to stop, but he wouldn't look at me. He just went on talking.

I actually felt like walking off in a huff, there and then – but a professional doesn't do that. I'd had worse audiences in the past, of course, but never in the grounds of Buckingham Palace.

A year later I found myself at a dinner for the British Film Institute. Sir Richard Attenborough was in the chair, and the royal guest was – yes, Charles. After the dinner, Dickie introduced us.

Charles shook my hand. 'I'm so sorry,' he said. 'I didn't realize you were going to be here, or I would have asked you to play for us.'

I couldn't resist it. I said: 'The last time I played, you weren't even listening. You talked all the way through it.'

Charles looked bemused. 'What? When was that?'

I told him: 'In your house.'

Attenborough was pulling frantic 'get out of here' faces at me behind his royal guest's back, but I ploughed on, starting to spell out the details in no uncertain terms. Charles raised an eyebrow in that quizzical expression he has made peculiarly his own, and said something like: 'Oh . . .' before in mid-sentence I was discreetly ushered away by an aide. At least I had got it off my chest.

A week later I was at another party at a friend's house.

Up came Vic Chapman, the popular and likeable press attaché to the Prince of Wales. 'Boy,' he said, without preamble. 'You really gave me a hard time.'

'What do you mean?' I asked.

'After that BFI dinner last week Charles said to me: "What did I do wrong? Why was Larry Adler so angry with me?" '

I told him the full story. Chapman said: 'Look, will you write a note to him to clear the air?'

So I went upstairs to the study, found some notepaper, and wrote a few short lines, put them in an envelope, and sealed it. Then I handed it to Vic.

'Give this to him,' I said.

'Thank you,' said the press attaché, presuming it was an apology. 'I'll make sure he gets it.'

I had written: 'I will not talk while Larry Adler is playing. Write this out one hundred times.'

To his great credit, the word came back that Prince Charles had found it extremely funny. But I still wouldn't lay any bets on my chances of an honorary knighthood.

Let me tell you about the Thursday Club. Prince Philip was a regular guest. It was a dining club for writers, journalists, actors and politicians, and I was a founder member back in the late 1940s when we got the whole thing together.

Arthur Christiansen, who would write his name into the ink of Fleet Street as the most famous editor the *Daily Express* ever had, was another. So were the eminent scriptwriter T.E.B. Clark, the photographer Baron, Peter Ustinov, the Cabinet Minister Iain Macleod, and other luminaries like the editors of *Tatler*, *Punch*, and sundry other organs of the Fourth Estate. My own organ, I carried in my pocket.

We would meet every Thursday for lunch at Wheeler's in Old Compton Street, the flagship of the famous restaurant chain that specializes in fish. Our meeting place: a private room on the second floor opposite what is now the Prince Edward Theatre but in those days was the London Casino. We sat at one long table under a sea-green ceiling, and there was a cuckoo clock on the wall above the fireplace behind the chair at the head of the table.

We would have a darned good meal costing us £10 a head, usually around twenty of us, and brilliant conversation. And each week we would invite a celebrity to join us.

It was all very jolly and informal, totally private, and everyone knew they could relax because nothing said within those panelled walls would ever get into the papers.

If anyone ever became the slightest bit pompous, the rest of us would all burst out into a spontaneous rendering of 'Lloyd George Knew My Father', which invariably had the desired effect of causing them to subside immediately.

One time I invited Rod Steiger as my personal guest. Mr Steiger happens to be a marvellous actor – but he knows it. He arrived in dark glasses, insisted on keeping them on, and started getting into his Method mode, declaiming from the head of the table as if he was striding the battlements at Elsinore. We got the distinct impression he was expecting everyone to ask for his autograph.

At a signal from Christiansen we all burst into song – and Mr Steiger became a human being again. Cruel? Not really. Just fun. And afterwards I had to write in the club book one hundred times: 'I will not bring Rod Steiger here again.'

On one notable occasion we held a winter dinner for Prince Philip. We always got on well – he called me Larry, I called him Philip. Although he was a regular, this was a special occasion, and he invited Prince Bernhard of the Netherlands along.

At one point during the meal Philip turned to him and said: 'You know, I really envy you. You can go anywhere you like, have girlfriends all over the world – and no one will take a blind bit of notice, because nobody knows what you look like. Whereas with me, I can't go anywhere without six detectives following me.'

Bernhard had to leave early to catch a plane back to his country. As he got up, Philip went down on his knees in front of all of us, salaamed to the floor, and said: 'Give my regards to Her Imperial Majesty.' I've always felt that Philip never did like having to walk a few paces behind the Queen . . .

That splendid actor James Robertson Justice was another member, complete with his great red beard and massive frame.

The discussions would often get quite heated. On one famous occasion I was on my soapbox about public schools, which I maintained were factories for manufacturing homosexuals.

James was sitting between Philip and myself. 'Oh Christ, Adler,' he boomed. 'Are you on that dreary hobby-horse of yours again?'

'Well, it's true – ' I said.

'Of course it's true,' said Justice in his foghorn tones. 'I went to Eton, and I was buggered in my first week there, in the dormitory with all the others watching. It did me no harm whatsoever.'

'Jimmy,' I said. 'It was different in those days. The whole school had to turn out to watch because of their motto: "Justice must not only be done, but must be seen to be done!"'

The whole table exploded in laughter, and I thought Philip was going to fall off his chair.

The college motto in fact is *Floreat Etona* – 'Let Eton flourish (or flower)'. For Jimmy, it was more *Defloreat Justice*.

Another founder member was Guy Middleton, a tall, urbane actor who specialized in playing smooth cads. Two days before he got married he held his stag luncheon with the club, and we all turned out in morning suits and striped trousers.

Philip was sitting next to the Marquis of Milford Haven. As we all sat down, he called across the table to Baron.

'You're a world-famous photographer,' he said. 'But we'll bet you £100 you can't take a picture of that cuckoo coming out of the clock at three o'clock.'

'Done!' said Baron, thinking he was on an easy bet.

He set up his tripod, pointed it at the clock, and finished his meal with one eye on the wall.

At two minutes to three he got up, and waited by the camera. With seconds to go, Philip and the Marquis suddenly jumped up, produced half a dozen cherry bombs, and hurled them into the fireplace.

Cherry bombs, for the uninitiated into such schoolboy pranks, are small red firecrackers the size of marbles, but they make the most hellish bang. That chimney hadn't been cleaned in twenty years, and when they went off the whole room was filled with soot and the sounds of choking and coughing as we made a rush for the windows and fresh air.

The cuckoo popped out, but no one could see it. Half a dozen detectives rushed in – they told us later they thought someone was trying to assassinate Philip. They found twenty refugees from the 'Black and White Minstrel Show' struggling to gulp in air. Baron lost his £100 – and paid up on the spot.

The sequel nearly led to an early divorce. I shouted above the general confusion: 'C'mon, fellers – everyone back to my place!' In those days I had a flat in Grosvenor Square. Unfortunately, I omitted to phone ahead and warn my wife.

Sally, bless her, had been doing a spot of spring cleaning. Philip and Milford Haven went ahead in the official car that was waiting downstairs, while the rest of us flagged down taxis. The bell went – and Sally, in headscarf and apron, answered the door to find Prince Philip and the Marquis of Milford Haven in full morning attire, faces speckled with black soot, standing there.

'Your husband was kind enough to invite us over

for a drink,' said Philip. Well, she had to let them
in. But I think I can pinpoint that moment when my
marriage started to dissolve . . .

I got into some very curious conversations at the
Thursday Club. We were ostensibly strictly stag.
But we broke the rule once – when Aristotle Onassis
was our guest of honour. The millionaire Greek
shipowner brought Maria Callas with him, and I
found myself sitting next to this very formidable
diva.

Somehow we got talking about children. She said
firmly: 'I believe that a disobedient child should be
beaten. What do you think, Mr Adler?'

'Well,' I said, 'I have three children, and in all my
life I have only hit one of them once.'

'Oh?' she said. 'Tell me – '

I explained how my son Peter, then aged eight,
had been playing with some other kids in a playground outside our hotel in Paris, where I had been
on tour. He was behaving stupidly, as kids do,
refusing to listen to me – and I had smacked him on
the side of the head, just once, in front of the other
youngsters.

He stared at me, then turned and ran back to the
hotel.

I followed him, feeling dreadfully guilty. In our
room, I found him lying on the bed, crying. 'Peter,'
I said. 'I've done something very wrong. Would it
make sense if you hit me back?'

He sat up. 'Could I?'

'Do you mind if I take off my glasses?' I said.
then: 'OK, go ahead!'

Does the Team Think? That was a show I appeared on – and there's Jimmy Edwards blowing his own trumpet – or French Horn – with little Arthur Askey having a tinkle (so to speak) and Tommy Trinder, who never did know when to take his hat off, trying to keep us all in time.

The King – Elvis, who else? But I didn't find his manager Colonel Parker too responsive.

My acting career was somewhat shorter than Ronald Reagan's, and I never did make it to President, either.

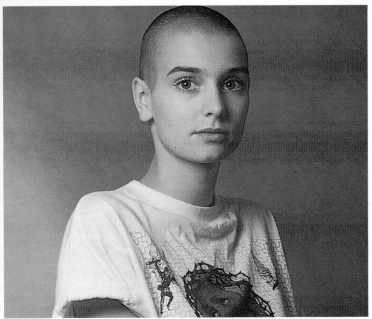

Top: Intense discussion with Esther Rantzen and husband Desmond Wilcox.

Above: Sinead O'Connor...

...and Kate Bush, just two of the ladies who helped me celebrate *The Glory of Gershwin.*

Above: The sign says QUIET, PLEASE. No chance when Dizzy Gillespie's around. It was Dizzy who led me astray and persuaded me to smoke marijuana for the first and only time in my life. Never again!

Above: Lisa Stansfield, a real honey, who sings *They Can't Take That Away from Me* on the Gershwin album. And who'd want to?
Opposite: With the amiable *Fiddler on the Roof* star, Topol.

Prince Charles – I told the future king to keep quiet while I was playing!

And – pow! He thumped me with his little fist, right on my cheek. Then he threw himself into my arms – and everything was fine, finished, end of drama.

La Callas stared at me in astonishment. 'You let your son strike you?' she said incredulously.

'Yes – '

'I have no son,' she said slowly. 'But if I had, and I invited my son to strike his mother – *and he did* . . . I would throw him to the ground and stamp my heel into his face!' And she meant it.

After that story, I found I didn't have too much more to say to that lady. She was a great, great artist. But I got an impression that the maternal instinct was definitely lacking.

8

Ingrid

*'You're not only ignorant, Larry. You're
proud of your ignorance!'*

Ingrid Bergman

I'm going to tell you now about Ingrid Bergman,
one of the great loves of my life. I fell for her on
sight – but didn't everyone? She told me once that
every single one of her leading men had been in
love with her.

The difference was that they didn't get as far as
the bedroom, and I did.

I'm actually a very romantic guy. I have to have
respect for the lady I'm going to bed with. I respect
women, I love them, and I hate it when people
make cheap jokes about women – even mothers-
in-law!

So it was wonderful that my affair with Ingrid
Bergman began like a story-book romance. The
dialogue could have come straight from a movie
script, except that this was real.

In the spring of 1945 I was on a tour with Jack

Benny and Martha Tilton, this time near the front lines in Europe. We arrived in Augsburg on a breezy March day, and had some time to kill before our concert party was complete. We were one woman short, but the top brass assured us that a 'name' actress was on her way, though nobody seemed to know what the name was.

We were staying in an unoccupied house they had requisitioned for us. It had everything, including a piano in the ground-floor living-room. That evening I was sitting alone, idly tinkling the keys, when this tall, breathtakingly beautiful woman walked in through the door and quietly sat down in an armchair facing me. I thought her face looked familiar, but I wasn't sure.

I finished playing, looked up and smiled at her. 'That was nice,' she said, in a voice that had a pronounced accent. A lovely voice, one that went with the face. 'What is it?'

'Just something I made up,' I told her.

'Is it published? What's it called? Have you written it down?'

No, I said, I hadn't written it down because I didn't know how to write music.

The lady pursed her lips in disapproval. 'You're very smug, aren't you?' she said severely.

'Smug?' I echoed. 'Just what is that supposed to mean?' People had called me a lot of things in my time, but smug wasn't one of them.

The lady bent her gaze on me. 'You're not only ignorant,' she said. 'But you're proud of your ignorance.' That was Ingrid Bergman. A challenge from the start. How could I *not* fall for her?

At that time Ingrid was at the peak of her career. She had starred in films that would become classics of the cinema. It was as if fame had attached itself to her like a pet dog and trotted obediently in her footsteps. Her radiance, strength and vitality increased with everything she did.

Three years previously she had made the unforgettable *Casablanca*, pipping Ann Sheridan to the post to play the lovely Ilse opposite Humphrey Bogart's cynical café owner Rick Blaine. A year later: *For Whom the Bell Tolls*, the opulent if overly solemn Spanish civil war drama with Gary Cooper that earned them both Oscar nominations.

The next year, the Oscar itself for *Gaslight* – the Victorian melodrama produced by my old friend Arthur Hornblow Junior. Then *Spellbound*, *Saratoga Trunk*, and *The Bells of St Mary's*, with Bing Crosby singing the title song as Father O'Malley and Ingrid as Sister Benedict, roles that gained them both nominations for the Academy Award that by now was starting to look somewhat familiar to Ingrid.

We began our affair a few days after that first meeting. Ingrid was a year younger than me, an orphan since early childhood whose single-minded ambition, fostered at the Swedish Royal Dramatic Theatre School, was to succeed in her chosen career.

I can't say that we wooed each other with heart-felt protestations and flowers, but for me it was a love affair unlike any other I would ever experience.

I loved her simplicity and directness. There was nothing coy about her, no teasing or coquetry. With this lady, you knew where you stood. Within hours I was apologizing for my smugness and promising to study musical composition when we got back to the States. Yes, ma'am!

To start with, we were constantly on the road to perform for the troops. We were thrown together by our work, which meant that we shared the same hostel, houses, apartments, or military quarters – wherever they could find us space. Later, after the war, we would be able to relax together and explore our love for one another more deeply.

Ingrid had joined our troupe, but had no idea what she was supposed to do. She had brought the script of a play with her called *Joan of Lorraine*. I told her to drop it: GIs preferred comic books to culture. Instead, I suggested she sang a Swedish folk song, with my harmonica backing her.

Being Ingrid, being stubborn, she would have none of it. At our next stopover in Kassel, north of Frankfurt, she suddenly halted in the middle of one of Lorraine's speeches, and ran off the stage with tears streaming down her face.

I peered out at the massed rows of GIs. Right below the stage, a group of goons were waving condoms they had blown up like balloons, and grinning all over their stupid faces.

'Hey,' I shouted, striding out on to the stage like the Caped Crusader. 'What a pity you guys can't find a better use for those!' I got away without being lynched, but I was mad as hell anyway and didn't care what I said.

Jack Benny and I worked on a sketch for Ingrid, a

send-up of *Casablanca* where he would take the
Humphrey Bogart role. Benny as the Bogey man?
But it worked.

Casablanca had been made in 1942. We got hold
of a script from Hollywood without any trouble, and
added some lines. In our version Ingrid was trying
to persuade Jack to leave his wife and run away
with her.

'You fool,' she cries, shaking Jack by the
shoulders like a bunch of old laundry. 'Can't you
see? This is bigger than we are – '

Jack's come-back line was supposed to be: 'You're
bigger than I am,' which may not look that brilliant
on paper but went a treat with the deadpan Jack
Benny delivery. The problem was, Ingrid *was* bigger
than he was – and it was one of those times when
Jack just broke up every time he reached that line.

It happens. But the result was that he never did
get it out. The only time that line was heard was the
night Jack went down with a cold and I had to take
over.

For me, no problem. Ingrid was bigger than me,
too, but I didn't care. I loved that lady, didn't I?

One of the nice gestures she made on that tour
was to take the names of various soldiers she met,
and promise to phone their parents or loved ones
when she got back to the States – a promise she
always kept.

Sometimes I felt as if I had known Ingrid all my
life, as if we had grown up together. Our love was
passionate, but it was more warm, tender and
caring than purely erotic. When the physical act was

over we would hold each other and talk far into the night, my own honesty matching hers, totally free, knowing we had no games to play.

But even then, I also knew that I could never marry her. I just could not beat her lust, her obsession, for her career. I knew if we ever did walk up the bridal path I would end up a few weeks later walking four paces behind Ingrid. She was the star, and I didn't think my own ego could cope with being Mr Ingrid Bergman.

By one of those strange strokes of fate, both our careers would fall apart at almost the same time. Mine because I was blacklisted in the infamous McCarthy witch-hunt. Ingrid's when in 1949 she deserted her husband Dr Peter Lindstrom, a dentist she had married twelve years previously, along with her daughter Pia, and ran into the arms of the Italian director Roberto Rossellini.

He left his wife, too, and their open liaison before they finally married both scandalized and titillated the public. It also led to a virtual boycott of their films in America, even the much-heralded *Stromboli*, in which Ingrid played a refugee who marries an Italian fisherman. Their controversial union produced not only films but a son and twin daughters. Poor Ingrid was even castigated in the US Senate, where she was called 'Hollywood's apostle of degradation' and a 'free-love cultist'. It took years for her career to recover.

I knew better. The Ingrid I loved, and still hold in warm memory, was as far removed from that description as the North and South Poles are apart.

We had our tiffs, of course. I think the worst was when I dared to criticize her performance in *Saratoga Trunk*, when she played a scarlet woman who turns up in New Orleans and falls for a cowboy (Gary Cooper) working on the local railroad.

Someone had shown up with a print of the movie, and Ingrid asked for it to be run just for the two of us in a screening-room in Nuremberg. It went on for two and a quarter hours, far too long. At the end she asked the fatal question: 'Well, Larry, what did you think?'

Now there are several replies to a question of this kind. You can look the person in the eye, and say, quite seriously: 'Ingrid, you've done it again!' Or: 'Ingrid' – catch in voice – 'I – I . . . just can't find the words.' Chances are, they'll walk away satisfied. I've seen it happen more than once with Hollywood directors, and it works a treat.

With Ingrid – fat chance. She was too direct herself, and besides, she could read me like a book. So I grasped the nettle, and told her what I thought. 'Ingrid, I'm sorry, but it's not a good part for you. It's all wrong. It's miscast – you look too healthy and too *Swedish* for the role. And it just doesn't come alive.' True diplomat, that's Larry. I suppose I could have added: 'Apart from that, it's fine,' but it didn't seem the right moment to crack jokes.

The critics would later agree with me. But Ingrid, so honest, so free of any kind of affectation, was also blind to the faults in that film. In fact, she thought it was the best work she'd ever done – and told me as much in icy tones. It was a week before she said anything nice to me.

Come to think of it, the only good thing about that movie was the height of its leading man. 'Coop' cut a great figure as a cowboy, rangy, drawling – and tall. Unlike another of her leading men she used to laugh over: Charles Boyer, the screen's 'great lover', who starred with her in *Gaslight*. 'He had to stand on a box to kiss me,' she recalled, giggling like a schoolgirl. 'And when we strolled together, they actually had to dig a ditch for me to walk in, and film us from the waist up.'

Boyer was one of the profession's true gentlemen, with a philosophy degree from the Sorbonne. Tragically, he took his life in 1978 with an overdose of drugs two days after the death of his wife. They had been married forty-four years.

We reached Frankfurt on the tour, and were invited to the US Officers' Club. There Jack Benny and I were forced into joining the dreaded game of 'Chugalug'. It's rugger-crowd stuff, as you may know, and was obviously dreamed up by a barroom drunk. A pint of beer is filled up, someone recites a few lines of doggerel, then everyone chants: 'Then *drink*, Chugalug! Chugalug!' and you have to down the pint in one, without even stopping to wipe the foam off your face.

For someone like me who doesn't drink, apart from the occasional sociable glass, it was sheer torture. But the officers had taken enormous trouble to make us welcome, and it would have been churlish to refuse. I managed to get my pint down

– and, more important, keep it down – and having proved I was one of the boys, I eased my way to the edge of the crowd.

I found myself standing next to an attractive woman who turned out to be General Eisenhower's chauffeuse. Her name, she said, was Kay Summersby. I told her that we were trying to get into Berlin, but that civilians were not yet being allowed in.

'Oh, I think it can be done,' she said. 'The thing to do is to see the General.'

'Eisenhower?' I laughed. 'Oh, yes? How on earth do we get to see Eisenhower?'

'Through me,' she said placidly. 'Excuse me for a minute.'

She went to the far corner where there was a phone booth, and was back two minutes later. 'You have an appointment with the General tomorrow morning,' she said briskly. 'Eleven o'clock.'

I heard later that it was common knowledge that she was having an affair with Ike, though – unlike today with the media, when no stone or sheet is left unturned – it never got into print.

Next morning Ingrid, Jack and I had breakfast together in the hotel where they had put us up. As we were finishing our coffee, a uniformed GI came up to the table, and saluted. The car was outside to take us to Ike. Jack and I got up, but Ingrid remained seated.

'Ingrid, come on. The car's here,' I said.

'No,' she said. 'I've changed my mind. You two go. You don't really need me.'

'For God's sake, Ingrid,' I exploded. 'You may never get a chance like this again. Don't you want to meet Eisenhower?'

She shrugged. 'I have nothing to say to him.' Oh dear. But that was Ingrid. And she meant it.

On the way to the Allied Command HQ in the I.G. Farben building, as the car picked its way through the rubble of a city that seemed almost totally destroyed, I started to worry. It occurred to me that Ike had granted us an audience purely to meet Ingrid Bergman, though maybe Jack and I carried enough clout to make us viable, too.

I was right. Eisenhower didn't keep us waiting. We were shown into his office by a uniformed aide, and shook hands. He looked over our shoulders. 'Just the two of you?'

We mumbled excuses for Ingrid's absence. Ike looked visibly upset, but did his best not to be obvious about it. We told him why we were there, to ask a favour. Could we possibly get into Berlin?

Ike reached for the phone on his desk. He got through to a General Parks, and told him to find a plane to take Mr Jack Benny, Mr Larry Adler and their party to Berlin, a.s.a.p. Then he put the phone back.

That had been quick, less than two minutes I'd say. There was no point in taking up the great man's time any longer. He had a peace to negotiate. We rose to go.

'Hold on,' said Ike. 'You fellows busy?' Not until our flight to Berlin. 'Good. Why not stay and have some coffee?'

Eisenhower seemed to enjoy talking to us. He was friendly and affable, and we chatted about the shows, the audiences we'd been getting, about golf. He had a rare presence about him that was a mix of a commander's authority and the shrewd down-to-earth personality that would charm his country into making him President.

Suddenly he was saying: 'I don't like this anti-Russian press. I don't like it at all.'

I had already met one general who in the bar of the Officers' Club had raised his glass in a toast: 'Here's to the next war against the Russkies!' I omitted to mention this little item to Ike. Instead I asked: 'How do you find them?'

'The Russians? Well, take General Zhukov. He's my opposite number. He comes to a meeting looking stiff and formal. I offer him a drink, crack a joke – and in no time he's a human being. They're not all that difficult, the Russians. You just have to know how to approach them.'

I asked him how he felt about the mounting campaign back home to run him for President. Ike frowned. 'Bad business,' he said. 'Sure, I'm aware of it – but why don't people read their history books? It has never worked that a military man has made a good President.

'I'm a graduate of West Point, and I'm trained to take my orders from a civilian commander-in-chief. I'll have nothing to do with it.'

He semed to mean every word. If Ike ever dipped into the history books a few years later, he might have remembered our talk.

But somehow I doubt it.

In the ruins of Berlin, we picked our way through the terrifying, depressing aftermath of war to locate Hitler's headquarters – not the bunker, but the Reichskanzlerei. It was a sobering sight. The shell of what had once been an imposing building reared out of the rubble like a rotting tooth. Gingerly Ingrid and I made our way up the shell-damaged staircase to the first floor, and out on to a stone balcony.

Had Hitler stood on this very spot, I wondered, looking out at crowds gathered below to cheer him in the early fever of the war? Now the walls were pock-marked with bullets, the windows no more than gaping black holes.

A few of our boys were standing on a mound of stones and earth below the balcony when I appeared. Recognizing Ingrid, they raised enthusiastic wolf-whistles – at least, I presumed they were for her. I gave them a wave, and one of them shouted: 'Give us a tune!'

Nothing loath, I perched on the edge of the balcony, and took out my harmonica. I looked over my shoulder at Ingrid, and raised an eyebrow. One of the show-stoppers we did together for the troops was the Gettysburg Address, with Ingrid reading it out and myself backing it with 'The Battle Hymn of the Republic'. I tell you, if that didn't give you goose-bumps, nothing would.

Now seemed as good a time as any for an impromptu performance, and she nodded back. The result earned us an extra cheer from the lads – and Ingrid, standing behind me, produced her camera and immortalized the moment for posterity.

Many years later I heard a recording that Margaret Thatcher made of that same address – and I like to think she was playing it for laughs, though somehow I doubt it. I've never heard such pomposity! She may have made a great Prime Minister, but after that recording, for me the initials PM will always stand for Pompous Maggie.

Ingrid and I kept our romance as discreet as possible. I had myself been married in 1938 – she was a vivacious model named Eileen Walser. I didn't want her to be hurt. Ingrid seemed to be stable enough in her own marriage to Peter Lindstrom.

In New York, and elsewhere in the States when we finally got home after the war, we always stayed in separate rooms. Same hotel, yes. But rooms on different floors. I didn't want to compromise her in any way, because she had her career at stake.

In Europe it was different. Once we stayed together at the famous Crillon Hotel in Paris, and that made me a little nervous. Its bar was a famous watering-hole for journalists, like the legendary Sam White, the Paris correspondent of the London *Evening Standard*. It would only have taken one eagle-eyed reporter to spot us, and the scandal would have hit the headlines across the globe.

Another tour was over, this one just after the peace treaty had been signed. We booked in for a week. 'Ingrid, we can't stay here too long,' I muttered, as the porter put our cases down in our elegant suite overlooking the square. 'Your husband

and my wife will wonder why we haven't come straight home.'

'Relax, Larry,' she said soothingly. 'I don't want to go home just yet.' We held each other close, in silence. At last she said: 'The war may be over, but it doesn't mean we have to stop seeing each other.'

We stayed ten days.

As I have intimated, Ingrid was a wonderful lover, but not a sex bomb. There was affection and warmth between us rather than great panting lust. She was a caring person, sheer joy, and she laughed a lot too.

That's always been the most vital part, if I can put it like that, of any relationship for me – shared humour. If you haven't got that, you're doomed. On the tours with Jack Benny, she would chide us: 'You two are children!' And maybe we were, at that.

One baking day in the North African desert Jack and I had written a parody of 'Oh, What a Beautiful Morning'. It went:

> Oh, what a hell of a morning,
> One hundred degrees in the shade.
> Oh, what a hell of a morning –
> It's even too hot to get laid!

When we tried it out on Ingrid, she shook her head sadly. 'Infantile,' she said, and walked off.

Jack and I consoled ourselves with the thought that Swedes don't have much of a sense of humour, anyway.

We talked seriously about marriage. The one big

difference between us in that quarter was that she was willing to leave her family life – no, not her career – and give up her husband Peter and her daughter Pia to marry me. I was too much of a coward to break up my family – by then I had not only a wife, Eileen, but three kids, Carole, Peter and Wendy (in that order).

Ingrid didn't like it. 'Come on, Larry, where's your courage?' she demanded. I had no answer.

Instead I wrote Ingrid a tune. I called it 'I Melt', a silly title really, but I meant it, and she knew it. The first time she heard it was when I broadcast it on the radio just for her – though nobody else ever knew. It was our secret song.

I had taped it for a programme going out from New York, coast-to-coast. I'd flown to Europe the same day, but I called her in California from London and told her: 'Listen to this station at noon. The song is "I Melt". It's for you.'

There were no lyrics. I never recorded it, because somehow it was too personal. To this day I can remember how it went – kind of a beguine tempo. Ingrid loved that song.

It was the last time I talked to her. Our affair lasted two years, and I think of great nights, great hotels, great dinners, great romance. But it couldn't last, and in the end we went our own ways.

At least I've got a song to remember her by.

9

Benny's from Heaven

> *'I think Larry Adler is absolutely fabulous!'*
>
> Joanna Lumley

The 1945 Ingrid Bergman/Jack Benny tour was my second USO tour with him. The United Services Organization was the American equivalent of ENSA, and I was proud to be asked to participate in its activities in 1943. Our ticket, courtesy of the US Air Force, would take us to theatres of war in Europe, North Africa and the South Pacific.

Jack was a lovely guy. OK, he was twenty years and four days older than me, but he treated me like a brother. His unpromising early career as a violinist became an integral part of his stage persona, the instrument his wooden fall guy, part of the image of the wise-cracking deadpan miser that brought laughter to millions over four decades.

Who can forget that hilarious gag when Jack is held up in the street? 'Your money or your life,' threatens the mugger. Long pause. 'I said: "Your money or your life!"' snarls the attacker.

'I'm thinking . . . I'm *thinking*!' cries Jack Scrooge. That's one gag that will live for ever.

Jack's timing was perfection personified. Aided by his black valet Eddie 'Rochester' Anderson, he would prolong every pause to its limit, and milk more laughs in utter silence than any other comic, living or dead.

The one person who could make Jack Benny laugh just by looking at him was George Burns. I saw it for myself one unforgettable evening at a plush dinner party hosted by the formidable Louis B. Mayer, the *capo di capo* of MGM, at his Bel-Air mansion.

After dinner the mogul ordered us upstairs to the music room to hear the cabaret he had put on specially for the night's entertainment: Jeannette MacDonald, no less, in her prime as the doyenne of the MGM box-office attractions.

I overhead Burns mutter to Jack as we went up the huge marble staircase: 'You know, Jack, this lady is the biggest star at MGM. It would be *very* bad taste on your part if you were to laugh while she's singing.'

We sat down in gilt chairs which had been placed around the walls, leaving a large space in the centre. The plump figure of Louis B. emerged in a dinner jacket, and held up both hands to call for silence. The room quietened. 'Ladies and gen'lmen,' he said in reverential tones. 'May I present a great lady: Miss Jeannette MacDonald!'

Applause. Lights lowered, apart from a beam shining on Jeannette's lovely face as she stepped out into the light. She began to sing – the 'Indian Love Call'.

'When I'm calling *you-oo-hoo-hoo*, *oo-hoo-hoo* . . .' Her voice rose to the rafters.

I saw George Burns across from me catching Jack's eye. I saw his lips move, miming: 'D-o-n't l-a-u-g-h!'

That did it. Jack's body started to shake uncontrollably. Then he went into spasms. Finally he doubled up, and burst out laughing.

He had to leave the room. And he was never invited back to darken the Mayers' doorstep again.

Jack would look in his dressing-room mirror and prepare himself to step out on to the world stage as vain, selfish and stingy. The real man was warm, generous, modest and mild-mannered. Anything for peace and quiet, that was his motto. I saw him angry just once.

We had set up our show on an open stage in Benghazi, which for the prospective tourist is a seaside hellhole in Libya facing out to the Gulf of Sirte. In those days it was a war zone. Today, I suspect nothing much has changed.

No one warned us about the sandstorms. This one blew up out of nowhere in the middle of a solo I was playing: Brahms's Hungarian Dance No. 5. It blew Brahms right back down my throat, seasoned with generous helpings of Sahara sand.

Connoisseurs say that Las Vegas sand is better, that it has a certain piquancy. I've tried them both, and I can assure you: there's nothing in it.

I came to the end of that show with my back

turned to the audience of troops, who were also suffering stoically in the cause of art. The boys sat on makeshift chairs or benches, some lined up on tanks that were clustered around like the boxes at the Albert Hall, only these ones had their guns presumably pointing in the general direction of Rommel somewhere over the horizon.

I had to change harmonicas twice. A sand-clogged harmonica somehow lacks resonance. A sand-clogged harmonica player lacks everything – except sand.

Ingrid Bergman had yet to join the gang. But Jack was up there giving his all on his violin, which also wasn't helped by the sand, along with our glamour girls in the hour-glass shapes of Martha Tilton, Wini Shaw (who sang 'Lullaby of Broadway' in the classic *Gold-diggers of 1935* musical) and Anna Lee.

We got through the show somehow, but it wasn't easy. After it was over we were escorted to a Red Cross tent where we sank down in relief at a trestle table for coffee and doughnuts to ease our parched throats.

A lieutenant wandered in, a burly redneck with piggy eyes and a uniform that looked two sizes too small. Without invitation, he sat heavily down on one of the chairs at our table, and greeted us in a Deep South accent straight out of *Gone with the Wind*.

'Hi-ya, fellers. Hi-ya, Jack.' He pronounced it 'Jay-yuk'.

'Hi,' Jack responded wearily. He was pooped.

'How come y'all didn't bring that Ro-chester along with ya?'

Jack told him that Rochester had other commitments back home.

Our new-found friend considered this for a moment. Then: 'That's a goddamn shame, pardon mah French. Back home in Tallahassee, m'wife and me, we listen in every Sunday night. But shee-*it*, man. That Ro-chester, he's ninety per cent of yo' show – '

'You wish we'd brought Rochester, eh?' Benny asked.

'Sure do. Not to say you ain't funny yourself, Mr Benny. But I'm just crazy 'bout that Rochester.'

'OK,' said Jack, and I didn't like the sudden steely glint in his eye. 'Now let's suppose we had brought him. He'd be sitting at this table with us. How would you like that?'

'Now you just hold on a minute,' said the lieutenant. 'Ah'm from the South – '

'That,' said Jack, 'is why I didn't bring Rochester.'

It was turning into one of those days. The sandstorm subsided, but it was too hot to sleep. I wandered out like a nomad into the night, and found myself on the beach. The sea was totally calm by now, washing gently against the brown sand. The Milky Way was wheeling overhead, the stars were diamonds on black velvet – and suddenly I felt drowsy. There and then I lay down in a sand dune, and was out like a light.

Suddenly I was hauled to my feet, literally, by a big hand on my collar. A torch was thrust into my face. A voice bellowed: 'Who the fuckin' hell are *you*?'

My head still fuzzy with sleep, I mumbled that I was an entertainer, that I was with the USO, and was in the middle of a tour.

'You're in the middle of a *minefield*! This is a military area!' the sentry shouted. I can't think why he didn't lower his voice, since his face was about six inches from my own. But now didn't seem the time to ask. He was a British sergeant, and the USO meant nothing to him.

'You got an ID card?'

No, I had not.

'OK, you're in an area where you shouldn't be, you've got no identification and you could have been shot. I'm taking you to the guard house. Now suppose you tell me your fuckin' name?'

'Larry Adler,' I said.

He stood back, shone the torch on me again, and said: 'Yeah? And I'm the fuckin' Duke of Windsor!'

In the guard house, while I poured sand out of my shoes, phone calls were exchanged. And finally I got to bed.

My wartime memories are a mix of farce and tragedy. I remember an airstrip at dawn, some-where in Europe, the planes standing like dark sentinels against the skyline, as their crews pre-pared to take off on a bombing mission. Where? Top-secret. But we knew. The target was the Ploesti oil field in Romania. The casualty rate would be high.

I played those men into their planes, knowing

that many of them would not be coming back.

Why was I there? For the camaraderie, the excitement, the feeling that we were playing some kind of modest part in the war effort, even if we never got as far as loading a rifle.

Certainly it wasn't the money. Jack and I were not paid a single penny for our personal war effort, nor did we expect to be. For some entertainers, war work was their main source of income. But we were doing well enough to make the trips as volunteers, and didn't need to take a salary.

However, we found that the USO had a strict rule that applied to everyone, from Jack Benny himself to the accompanist. The sum of $25 a week was to be paid for out-of-pocket expenses. Fair enough. They were given out in travellers' cheques. Over my strenuous objections I was elected to hand them out, and keep the record.

The result was that whenever anyone in our troupe needed money I would simply give them a cheque and as often as not omit to record it. When we finally flew back to the States, a po-faced military accountant in Washington asked for my expense list.

I stared at him blankly. 'What list?'

'You have paid out more than $1,000, and have no receipts,' he said coldly. 'Where are they?'

'Look,' I said. 'You got me into this in the first place. You are acting as if you seriously expect me to pay you this money out of my own pocket.'

It was the first and only time he smiled. 'You've got it in one.'

I paid.

We had our share of laughs, and a few tears too. And moments of high drama. In Accra, we found a renegade general who took a liking to us, and commandeered a C-47 cargo plane to fly us around the various bases in Africa where we were due to perform. Transport had been a trifle uncertain, to put it mildly, and this made the rest of that trip a joy.

In 1943 Billy Wilder had made a wartime drama called *Five Graves to Cairo*, a spy thriller set in a desert hotel in North Africa with a bunch of British spies trying to destroy Rommel's supply dumps. It was most noted for the appearance of the masterly Erich Von Stroheim, no less, as Rommel.

So I suppose it was inevitable that our plane should be dubbed *Five Jerks to Cairo*, an insignia painted triumphantly on the nose in the space normally reserved for pin-up pictures of Betty Grable.

Flying up to Lagos for a fresh date with the troops, we flew near a military base, and our crew received an urgent signal to land. The airstrip was small – too small. We overshot, screeched to a halt with our nose embedded in a clump of thorn bushes, and were generally bounced about. By luck, there were no serious injuries, just a few bruises and a lot of shredded nerves.

A grinning army sergeant loomed up as we descended the steps, considerably shaken and stirred. 'Hi, folks,' he said genially. 'There's no real problem, so don't worry. But the guys knew Jack

Benny was on board, and they want to see the show. OK by you?'

I nearly burst a blood-vessel. These jerks could have killed the lot of us. Jack, being the good-natured slob that he always was, went ahead with the show.

Me, I was hopping mad. I refused to go on, and my harmonica stayed in my pocket. Maybe that shows what a bastard I can be.

War zones . . . revolutions . . . I've had my share. And survived. In 1951 I found myself in Korea, in that depressing war where national servicemen shivered in an alien land in a conflict without any real rhyme or reason that they could understand.

But I did my bit. They had me hopping from trench to trench in sub-zero weather. It was so cold that I was warned to warm up the harmonica before playing it, or it would freeze to my lips. Nice thought! I may be Hot-Lips Larry, but this was ridiculous.

That tour was for the British Commonwealth Division. Unlike the US military, who never allowed me to venture near the front lines, the British took me so close to the enemy that I expected to be playing request numbers for the Chinese. On the other hand, maybe they *wanted* the enemy to hear me. To really clinch it, I could always have shouted a few jokes through a megaphone across the muddy trenches and brought the war to a speedy close.

In 1955 I was on a concert tour of the Far East.

From Djakarta I flew in a tiny plane across the Flores Sea to Makassar, an old fishing port that looks out across the Straits to Borneo.

I was met at the airport by a very polite man in a tropical suit who said he was the 'concert reception committee', and would I care to join him for a nice lunch at the airport.

The lunch wasn't particularly nice, and I wasn't particularly hungry, but it seemed churlish to refuse so I ate it anyway. Afterwards I suggested that we headed for town.

'Oh no, Mr Adler. We can't do that yet.' He looked quite alarmed at the idea. 'That is why we prepared lunch for you at the airport. We must wait for the army.'

I've had some pretty good escorts in my time, but even I was impressed by this rolling out of the red carpet. 'A military escort,' I said, envisaging a procession, colourful uniforms, pipes and kettle drums. 'That's nice.'

'Not really, Mr Adler,' said my host. 'You see, sir, Makassar is surrounded by guerrilla bands. We are having something of a revolution, which of course I very much regret. If the army does not take us into Makassar, we would simply not *get* into Makassar.'

Nobody in Djakarta had said anything about a revolution before I left. And indeed they did put me into a Jeep, with an armoured personnel carrier and two other military vehicles for company. We roared along the coast road at such a rate of knots that I scarcely had time to draw breath to do my harmonica justice. I was out of that place the next day – and

I managed to refrain from telling any antimacassar jokes.

Heat is another source of trouble to a musician. If my mouth organ wasn't about to freeze to my face in a Korean trench, it would be in danger of slipping out of my hands with the perspiration that was flowing from every pore.

In Bombay I had to change harmonicas after every two or three numbers. The reeds were sticking, probably from the humidity. The chromatic slide – by which I get my sharps and flats – would go in to the instrument all right. But then the spring would jam, and it wouldn't come out again.

After the interval, someone had the bright idea of putting an electric fan on either side of me, blowing right in my face. It stopped me perspiring – but I went down with a cold that lasted a week.

And for anyone thinking of taking up this wonderful instrument, be warned: the harmonica *can* fight back! You don't believe me? In that case I have to tell you about my first appearance at the London Palladium. Showing off as was my occasional wont, I was trying very hard to impress a young lady sitting in the front row of the stalls.

The 'Bolero', what else, for maximum effect? On the grand climax I swept the harmonica across my face for the great swooping finale with such bravura that I knocked a piece out of my front tooth. I still have the slight gap there, to this day.

The only good thing about that little incident was that the girl in question was Eileen Walser. And that to prevent me from further self-destruction, she married me.

Harmonica playing sounds like one disaster after another – but that, of course, is a slight exaggeration. Those heady, sometimes hairy days of worldwide concert tours – in peace and war – brought me in contact with so many places, so many faces, that sometimes I feel I lived more in a month than many people do in a lifetime.

By the end of the 1950s I had completed five tours of Israel, two tours of Japan, India, Malaya, Pakistan, Hong Kong. Three visits to Australia and New Zealand. My passport looked like Picasso's notebook.

I made a point of visiting hospitals wherever I could, walking around the beds playing to the patients. During World War II, I often played to disturbed soldiers in the psychoneurotic wards of military hospitals.

In New Guinea, I was at the end of one ward playing 'Begin the Beguine', when I was interrupted by a young soldier sitting in a chair nearby.

'Hey, buddy,' he called out. 'Do you have to tap your foot like that while you play?'

I said no, I didn't have to.

'Well, cut it out. I don't like it. It disturbs me.'

I apologized, and went on playing. He interrupted me.

'Hey, buddy. What d'ya keep swaying from side to side for? A guy could get drunk just lookin' at you!'

I explained that I was totally unaware that I was

shifting around. A nurse hurried over to the soldier. 'Don't be rude to Mr Adler,' she reprimanded him. 'He's trying to entertain you.'

'Look, lady,' he said. 'I'm nuts, ain't I? I'll tell him what I think.'

After I finished he gave me a few slow handclaps. Then he beckoned me over.

'Did you hear what I said to that dame?' he asked me. I nodded. He looked up at me: 'You agree? Do you think I'm nuts?'

'Well,' I said, 'if you want to know, I think you're the first truthful man I've met on the base.'

He held out a hand. 'Shake, buddy. We understand each other. What's your rank?'

'No rank,' I told him. 'I'm a civilian.'

'Come on, now,' he protested. 'I can see the officer's tabs on your shirt. What's your rank?'

'I told you, no rank,' I explained. 'I'm a forces entertainer, and they require us to wear military uniform out here. Then if we get captured we're treated as officer prisoners-of-war. Otherwise we might get shot as spies. In fact I've got no rank. I'm just a plain civilian.'

He stared at me incredulously. 'You mean nobody *made* you come out here?'

'No,' I said.

'I've got bad news for you, buddy,' said my new friend. 'You belong in this ward!'

In 1973, after the Yom Kippur War, I went to Israel again. But this time I was only going to play in hospitals. There had been heavy casualties. One thousand dead in Israel is like one hundred thousand in the US.

At the Hadassah Hospital in Jerusalem I played for a soldier who was in a private room, covered in plaster-of-paris from head to foot. He looked like the Invisible Man, but he was able to speak through a hole in the plaster-cast by his mouth.

He told me that before the desert wár had put him there he had been a musician. 'I used to play clarinet, trumpet and harmonica,' he said. 'Now I can't.'

'Of course you can't, I said, eyeing the mummy-like figure. 'But in a few months they'll take all this crap off and you'll be able to play again.'

'It isn't that, Mr Adler,' said the soldier. 'I smoke too much.'

Along the corridor I was taken into another private room. The blinds were drawn so that the young man lying in the bed lay in quiet, soothing shadow. He could only have been nineteen, and there wasn't a mark on him that I could see.

'What's wrong with him?' I found myself whispering to the nurse.

'He's in shock,' she answered. 'He was brought down from the Golan Heights a month ago. Please play for him. I have to tell you that you won't get any reaction, and you'll think he won't hear you. But we believe he does. So please will you try?'

I played 'Summertime'. The boy lay there, with no sign that he had heard. The nurse signalled me: one more. I shrugged, but went ahead. It is actually very hard to play to a person who gives absolutely no response.

I played 'Claire de Lune', which I had played in a film and seemed to be the one that most people asked for. When I came to the last note, and the echoes faded, the soldier's lips suddenly moved.

The nurse bent over him, then looked up, her face radiant. 'He *hears* you!' She was trying to suppress her excitement. 'And he asks you if you'd play something classical.'

I tried to act nonchalant. 'Ask him what he'd like.'

The kid spoke, quite clearly this time.

'Beethoven,' he said.

'Beethoven wrote several things,' I said gently. 'Which would you like?'

He wanted 'Ode to Joy', the finale of the Ninth Symphony. I began to play the famous *Alle menschen wurden bruder*, and as the music filtered out into the corridor other soldiers, some in wheelchairs, some on crutches, came into the room and started to sing it.

Then something else happened. The boy sat up in his bed, and he began to sing, too.

I turned away. I was close to tears, and I didn't want him to think that I was pitying him.

Before leaving Israel, I checked back with the hospital. There was no relapse. That incident had started a full recovery.

I told you harmonicas have a voice of their own.

10

Witch-hunt!

*'Adler, you're a pain in the ass. Anyone
ever tell you that?'*

Humphrey Bogart

There are some things in life you wish had never
happened, and this is one of them. It left a stain on
my career – and a sour taste in my mouth that I still
can't altogether erase.

I'm talking about the McCarthy witch-hunt of the
1950s that drove a nation into hysteria, caused more
than one suicide and turned friend against friend
before it was finally exposed for what it was: a sham
based on the power-mad ravings of a megalomaniac.

Joseph Raymond McCarthy – 'Call me Joe' – was
elected to the US Senate in 1947 at the age of thirty-
nine, and started leaving his grubby fingerprints
around from day one. When he made it to chairman
of the permanent subcommittee on investigations
and really started throwing his weight around – and
that of anyone who got in his way – he instituted
public hearings that were the modern equivalent of
the old Star Chamber.

We don't need a history lesson here. Suffice it to say that Senator Joe pilloried top army officials, public personalities and the world of show business with accusations, mainly unsubstantiated, that they were goddamn Commies who needed to be exposed. The Red-under-the-bed mentality caught fire and spread like a virus.

Military? Fine, let them fight back. Public figures? OK, let them say their piece. Show business? That's where I came in.

First of all, let's get one thing clear. I never voted Communist in my life. I was a Democrat. Whatever one's political leanings, from red to pink to blue to a lighter shade of pale, they can shift like the sands. Like my religion, my politics have only followed one god: *truth*.

I had friends, and still have, who were Communists. I was never attracted to the Communist Party, but it didn't stop me from talking politics with my friends in the business far into the night if we felt like it. But the simple fact is that I'm too much of a rebel to toe any party line.

I can trace the source of my political troubles back to three events: a dinner in San Francisco in 1946, a visit to Washington with Humphrey Bogart and other members of the First Amendment Committee we had formed, and playing the Roxy Theater in New York in 1948 with my old tap dancing pal Paul Draper.

At the famous Mark Hopkins Hotel in San Francisco one night in 1946, I was invited to play at an advertising function, full of veeps (vice-presidents, right?) in dinner jackets and wreathed in cigar smoke. But they also asked me to say a few words.

Being Mr Subtlety, I launched into a tirade against advertising – it created a false demand for commodities that were neither wanted nor needed, I informed them. I went further. Getting into my stride, I castigated their campaigns to get people to smoke or drink alcohol. Or to use some product because it promised sexual allure: Love Potion Number Nine, and there would be a wife or husband waiting at the end of the fantasy rainbow.

As you might suspect, that was lead-balloon time. The applause, such as it was, proved to be desultory – and that's putting it grandly. I was sent a magazine called *Aware*, in which I was described as a fellow traveller parroting the Communist Party line.

That was news to me, but in those high-strung political days it was news I could do without.

Next I met Humphrey Bogart. Our initial meeting was not exactly one you would describe as a social success, or a great meeting of minds. Bogey was smashed out of his skull, and tried to pick a fight from the moment he set eyes on me – and I hadn't even played him a note from my harmonica.

His friends all adored him, of course. That lovely feisty lady Lauren Bacall, who had married him the previous year and must have had the patience of a saint, was there too, at a party given by Lewis Milestone, who had carved his name into cinematic history in 1930 with *All Quiet on the Western Front*.

One guest was Jeff Cassells, a French screen-writer who had a party trick: he ate glass! That man would tuck away lightbulbs or wine glasses, always doing the gallant thing by asking permission of his hostess first, scrunching them up with obvious relish, while the rest of us winced and squirmed and tried to blot out the hideous sounds.

There were around fifty of us, enjoying a buffet dinner in the splendid Milestone mansion in Beverly Hills. After supper, things started to liven up. Cassells did his glass-chomping act, ignoring the cries of mock disgust, and received a rousing cheer as the last sliver disappeared.

Desi Arnaz and Eddie Albert gave an impromptu concert, singing Mexican folk songs together in soft close harmony. It was beautiful to listen to.

Suddenly there was the most almighty crash, and in staggered Bogart, blood running in rivulets down his chin.

He hung in the doorway, and pointed a red-stained finger into Cassells's face as he shouted: 'You son-of-a-bitch! I can eat more glass than you can!'

Bogey had smashed his fist into the full-length mirror in the hall outside, taken pieces of glass and tried to eat them. All he did was succeed in cutting his mouth to bits.

Bacall and some friends persuaded him to let them take him to the nearest hospital. As he was escorted past me I made the slight mistake of saying: 'I think you should apologize to Mrs Milestone.'

'Wha-at?' He turned his face my way, tried to focus, and bestowed his most ferocious glare on me. 'Whaddaya say – ?'

'And I think you should perhaps replace her mirror – '

His friends got him out of there before he could do any more damage, either to me or to the furniture. But I had made an enemy without even being introduced.

A few months later I was holding court with my wife Eileen to some friends at Chasen's Restaurant, a top Hollywood haunt for the stars, when Bogart suddenly loomed up out of nowhere.

He was staggeringly drunk. 'Fellas,' he announced, 'I'm giving a birthday party for Phil Baker in the private dining-room. He knows you're out here, and he wants you to join him and have some booze. Come on in, huh?'

Phil Baker was a well-known stage and radio comic, though personally I only had a passing acquaintance with him. At the table, our main course had just arrived.

'Bogey,' I said, as diplomatically as I could. 'We're in the middle of dinner – '

'F--- that!' said the great actor. 'Who gives a shit? Skip the goddamn dinner. Come on, for Christ's sake – it's Phil's birthday.'

I thought quickly. Bogart could be an ugly drunk. 'We can't leave in the middle of dinner,' I said. 'Look, we won't have dessert or coffee. We'll come in for a drink then. OK?'

He nodded, but didn't look too happy about it, and went back to the private dining-room.

Twenty minutes later he appeared at the far end of the restaurant. His voice carried across the room like someone hurling rusty nails. 'What the hell kind of fair-weather friends *are* you guys? Your pal's in here – it's his *birthday*, for Christ's sake. And just look at you, sittin' there guzzling. You oughta be *ashamed* of yourselves!'

Partly to stop the tirade, mainly to avoid a scene, we made the mistake of leaving our half-eaten meal and filing after him into the private room at the rear. Inside was a small, well-stocked bar. Bogey poured a large whisky and waved it at me. 'Here, have this!'

I refused. Second mistake. Bogey took it personally. He put an arm on each side of me so that I was pinned against the bar.

'Adler, you're a pain in the ass. Anybody ever tell you that?' he growled in a slurred voice. 'Because that's what you are, a pain in the ass. D'you want to know why?'

I didn't, but I was going to hear anyway.

'I'll tell you why.' His face was almost against mine. 'It's because you call yourself a liberal. That's a lot of horse-shit. You're not a liberal at all, you're a f---ing phoney.'

I tried to ease out, but he kept me pinned. 'You stay right where you are. You know why you're a phoney? Listen, I hate blacks. So do you, but you won't admit it because you're a phoney. I hate 'em, but I'll admit it. So who's a real liberal, you or me?'

He peered blearily around the room. 'And I'll tell

you something else. I hate Jews, and I know you're one.' It was my turn to peer past him to where Lauren Bacall stood. She had been born Bette Joan Perske. Bogey followed my gaze. 'OK, sure, I married one. That don't make no goddamn difference; I hate 'em. And so do you, but you won't admit it because you're a phoney. I'll admit it. So who's the real liberal, huh? You or me?'

He grabbed my lapel. 'What kinda guy *are* you, anyway? You come crashin' into my party, drink all my liquor . . .'

This time I managed to extricate myself, and turned to Eileen. 'Come on,' I said tersely. 'We're leaving.'

While we were waiting outside for the attendant to bring round our car – there was Bogart again. He seized my hand in a crushing grip.

'Jesus, Adler,' he said. 'What are we fighting about? We're both on the same side!'

What can you say?

Bogey and I next met at the house of Ira Gershwin on Roxbury Drive. It was in response to an emergency call. Nineteen writers had been subpoenaed to appear before the Senate House Committee on Un-American Activities in Washington, invitations courtesy of Senator Joe McCarthy.

The question they would be asked has been written into history: 'Are you now or have you ever been a member of the Communist Party?'

We sat around Ira's house discussing the implications, and the possible far-reaching effects. It would obviously affect the movie industry. Who knew where it would end? The director John Huston brought up the First Amendment to the Constitution, part of the Bill of Rights, which we believed guaranteed free speech and would thus forbid such a question being asked. That day we formed the First Amendment Committee, and decided to fly to Washington as a group to protest on behalf of the writers.

Others in the group that day included Danny Kaye, Gene Kelly and Frank Sinatra. We met again at Romanoff's restaurant to finalize our plans. Charlie Einfeld, the publicity chief at Warner Bros, proposed that we should charter a plane to make the trip. It would be expensive. We could try canvassing our friends to raise the money.

Bogart, sitting at one end of the table, suddenly spoke up. Looking straight at me, he said: 'I haven't got any friends. I meet people, but I get nasty with them, and I get into fights. So I'm no good to you.'

It was pure self-pity, of course. Bogey had a load of friends, and in fact had only joined our committee because one of them – his old pal from the *African Queen* days, John Huston – had helped form it. If Bogart had any convictions, I never heard him express them.

But he was on the plane with us when we flew to Washington, and posed in the group on the airplane steps for press photographs when we arrived. Sadly, he was the first to cave in. Without any warning, he astounded us by issuing a public statement, apologizing for having gone to Washington, insisting that he was no sympathizer, and calling himself 'a foolish and impetuous American'.

Bogart's cop-out defeated the whole purpose of our trip. Other big names followed, including Gene Kelly, Danny Kaye and Frank Sinatra, loudly disowning the group they had joined. Those of us who didn't, stood out like carbuncles.

My third sip from the poison political chalice took place in New York a few months later. I was still finding work without too much trouble, touring the country with Paul Draper in our music-and-dance act. This time we were at the Roxy as live supporting acts to an anti-Communist movie called *I Led Three Lives*, a low-grade thriller about an ex-Red who turned FBI informer. Outside, left-wing groups picketed the theatre, while inside we did our best in the highly-charged atmosphere to keep the show going and radiate good cheer and jollity.

One number that Paul performed was a dance called 'Political Speech'. He walked a tightrope, kissed imaginary babies in prams, and generally lampooned all the politician's clichés. Perhaps it wasn't the most tactful number to retain in the programme in view of the current state of affairs, but he kept going. Until one evening, during the 'Political Speech', someone booed. As these things do, the booing spread.

What did I do? I marched out and told the audience that if they saw anything in Paul's number to boo, they might as well boo me too. So they did, joyously and with abandon. It was so loud they probably heard it in the street outside, and all the way to Times Square!

It was picked up in the right-wing *Journal-American*, where columnist Igor Cassini took a swipe at us for 'selling Red propaganda' from the stage. The thing started to snowball.

A lady named Hester McCullough spotted the item, and wrote to the *Greenwich Times*, where we had been booked to play a date. We were, she insisted, pro-Communist. Money paid to us would go to Moscow and be used against the American way of life. She never actually called us Communists, which would have implied membership of the Party, but kept the accusations vague, and therefore almost impossible to disprove.

I was never hauled up before the Un-American Activities Committee, nor was I grilled by Senator McCarthy. It would have been an interesting confrontation. But our agents, William Morris, told us bleakly that if we did not sign a non-Communist affidavit or sue Mrs McCullough for libel, we'd be blacklisted. We sued.

While the case was pending – and that meant months – the atmosphere of hostility and fear deepened. A book appeared: *Red Channels*, naming two thousand show business artists, with a list of the organizations and places where they had performed. Anything with a sniff of left-wing spelled trouble. That was all, just names and organizations. But that book was deadly.

If you were listed, you had to 'clear' yourself – which basically meant naming names and degrading yourself in public before a committee. It happened to Edward G. Robinson, John Garfield,

Judy Holliday, Elia Kazan, Sterling Hayden, Larry Parks and many more.

Red Channels was published in alphabetical order. Guess whose name led the list! A for Adler, right in one. I was on the blacklist from then on.

At the height of the hearings I bumped into Edward G. Robinson on Broadway. He had already found himself blacklisted even before being called to face Senator Joe, guilty before being tried. Finally he appeared twice in front of the committee. It was just after the second hearing that I saw his small, burly figure walking slowly down Broadway. He had aged visibly, and looked shattered.

Edward G. was a good man, erudite, articulate, and the possessor of one of the finest art collections in the world. Every time I set foot in his house on the corner in Beverly Hills I would marvel at the quiet dignity of the place, with its dark wood panelling and antique furniture, somehow a reflection of the man himself. It was only a pity that he had to sell that magnificent collection to pay for his divorce from his actress wife Gladys, after twenty-nine years of marriage.

'Eddie – ?' He looked terrible.

We stood there on the pavement, and I looked into that wonderful face and didn't have to read between the lines on it to see desperation there.

'Larry! Have you read my testimony?'

No, I hadn't seen it in the papers. He took my elbow, and led me into the lobby of a nearby hotel. In a quiet corner, he motioned me to sit down in an armchair before he reached into an inner pocket and almost guiltily produced a sheaf of papers. 'Here – read this.'

It was harrowing. The committee had put him on the rack, made him abase himself, denounce his own feelings, virtually his own life. The testimony could have come straight out of the Moscow trials of the intelligentsia of decades ago.

I felt physically sickened to read it. Tears sprang into my eyes, and when Eddie saw how moved I was, he broke down and wept.

'Larry, you see what they did to me? It was dreadful. But – I'm working again! You must do the same thing – .' Indeed, he had crawled, he had been cleared, he had emerged with a clean bill of health. And perhaps a load on his conscience that he would carry for the rest of his life.

'Eddie, I can't.' I looked at him. 'I'm not condemning you. But . . . it's just not for me.'

'Larry, get back to work!' Eddie tapped my knee with an urgent finger. 'You're an artist – people should hear you. Say whatever they want you to say. The main thing is – *get back to work*! Don't let those bastards stop you. You've got to do it, Larry.'

But I couldn't. For Eddie, it served its purpose and got him back before the cameras. But he was ashamed at having kissed the asses of little men unworthy to be in the same room with him.

The blacklist started to bite. Doors slammed shut on all sides. I was able to perform a few dates, but my diary grew thinner by the week.

The irony was that I never put political content of any kind into my appearances. I felt it was wrong.

People had come to hear a mouth organ, not a political speech. I once had a fall-out with Paul Robeson over this.

If he could have stayed with 'Old Man River', that would have been fine in my book. Instead he made several trips to the USSR, and became increasingly enchanted with leftist ideology in his battle to improve the rights of blacks in the United States. He even received the Stalin Peace Prize in 1952.

Paul loaded his recitals with politics. 'It's your right to do so – but play fair!' I told him. 'You've got to advertise that Paul Robeson will sing – but will also speak.'

Robeson simply smiled that wonderful grin of his, and said: 'You do it your way, Larry. I'll do it mine.'

My big mouth is forever open and always will be. In St Louis I was invited to lecture at a national conference of Christians and Jews. The first question seemed primed to throw me. A girl of fifteen stood up, giggled, and asked: 'What do you think of the Communists?'

A ripple ran through the hall. I could have evaded the question with an off-the-cuff joke. Instead I told them that what I thought of the Communists was not important – the rights of the Communists were. They were a legal party, they could put up candidates in an election; even in that tense political climate, they could vote. Next day the St Louis *Globe-Democrat* headline read: COMMUNISTS HAVE RIGHTS, SAYS ADLER. That's all I needed.

Things grew steadily worse. Trying to keep my

integrity – and earn enough to pay the bills – was like swimming in cement. The work just dried up.

Finally the libel case came to court in Hartford, Connecticut. It lasted five weeks. In that time, American law being what it was, various columnists – or calumnists, dare I suggest – had branded Paul and myself as moral lepers, called on us to be deported, and generally given us somewhat unfavourable publicity. Press cuttings like that, I can do without.

Witnesses sprang out of the woodwork to defend us. A certain Colonel Stevens, who had been in British Intelligence during the war, had investigated me for clearance before I could do my tour of the Middle East. He offered to fly down from Montreal, where he had retired, to testify on my behalf. We gladly accepted, and his goodwill and honesty must have counted for a lot.

Others didn't spring out quite so readily. My old friend Jack Benny invited me over to his house, and explained that his business manager had advised him: *'At all costs – don't appear!'* His sponsors wouldn't like it. He was very distressed to have to tell me – 'But what can I do, Larry?'

'You could play your violin for me outside the court,' I said, trying to lighten his load. 'But don't lose any sleep over it, Jack, I wasn't planning to ask you anyway. I wouldn't have wanted to put you on the spot.' I meant it. I knew how vulnerable he was.

During the case, we never denied our left-wing stance. To many a mid-Westerner at that time, anything leftish was a goddamn Commie, or worse.

Even though to file the suit in the first place I had been forced to swear that I was not, nor ever had been a Communist.

Oddly enough, by the time the case wound up, the ink in many of the writers' pens had turned from vitriol to honey. They were actually writing 'observation' pieces in our favour, so much so that I went out of my way to warn one scribe on the right-wing *World-Telegram* that he could lose his job.

'Fuck 'em,' he said. 'From where I sit, you guys are being railroaded. That's how I see it, and that's the way I write it.'

If only he had been sitting on the jury. Eight men, four women, and that's the numerical way they voted. Eight to four – *against* us.

It would be another four years before Joseph McCarthy was discredited, censured and shown for the misguided bigot that he was. Which is putting it kindly. By which time the damage was done, and my career had taken its plunge into the abyss.

The ripples would go on for more years than that, eventually petering out on the shifting sands of public apathy. In the end it was my music that counted, and my harmonica stayed as bright and breezy as ever.

Meantime, I turned my back on America and headed for my new home – Britain.

11

Anyone for Tennis?

*'Larry is a tennis freak. I want to get him
in a photo with Pat Cash and Ivan Lendl.
Then I can call it Cash, Czech and Freebie.'*

Victor Lownes

Victor Lownes *is* right. I am a tennis freak. I have
been going at it (tennis, I mean) hammer and tongs
with the former *Playboy* chief for years. No quarter
given or asked. No mercy. No prisoners. On the
morning of my eightieth birthday I was on the
indoor court with him at my club in Paddington,
and I'll be there again today.

I discovered tennis in Hollywood, where else?
Deals are done over the net, or over a cooling beer
afterwards by the pool in country clubs or on private
courts in expensive acres of Bel-Air.

I was a member of the Beverly Hills Club, where
you find actors like Burt Lancaster, Charlton Heston
and Gene Kelly warming up on the courts – and
believe me, they're good players. Charlie Chaplin
would call me for a game, and he was no mean
exponent either.

One Saturday afternoon he phoned my house.

'Larry, can you get up here right away to make a fourth? Bill Tilden has dropped out. We're one short.'

Tilden was probably the greatest tennis player in the history of the game. When he drops out, who do you call? Larry Adler, of course.

I drove along Sunset Boulevard and turned in to Bel-Air, the most expensive square mile in the world. Driving through the green shrubbery that lined the driveway to Chaplin's house on Summit Drive, I could hear the sounds of racquet on ball.

Three people were knocking up on the private court. Chaplin was playing against a man and a woman, and as I pushed open the gate he simply motioned me to join him, without even the courtesy of an introduction.

I waved a vague hand in the direction of my opponents, called out a cheery: 'Hi!' and started playing. The lady across the net had her hair combed untidily back, wore blue shorts and a loose singlet, no socks and black plimsolls. The man had a black shirt, long slacks, a weird moustache, and he couldn't hit a ball.

As we knocked up, it was obvious that Chaplin was the best player. He had incredible anticipation, never seemed to run for the ball, but was always on the spot when it landed. I came a close second. The court surface was cork, very springy and easy on the feet. After a few minutes, the lady called out: 'Shall we play a set?' And I recognized that voice, then the face.

Greta Garbo. Her partner was Salvador Dali.

Well, Charlie and I whopped them, which perhaps wasn't a gentlemanly thing to do. But afterwards we sat sipping iced tea around his pool, and Garbo made it clear she bore us no malice. Out of costume, out of make-up, she still had exquisite bone-structure. But, unless you looked carefully, a face that would get lost in a crowd.

I admired Chaplin, of course I did. But there was one comic I admired even more: Buster Keaton. Why? Because he was a master of understatement. And he never begged the audience: *'Please love me!'* Chaplin did.

Another genius of comedy was Harold Lloyd, who seemed to take his life in his hands in every movie he made. He once said to me: 'People talk about my courage – but where on earth do you think the cameraman was?'

In one of our chats around his pool, Chaplin gave me an insight into his comedy.

'You've seem my film *The Gold Rush*?' Of course I had. 'Do you remember the scene where I'm walking along a mountain path, and a bear emerges from the forest and starts to follow me?'

I nodded. Yes, I recalled that scene. Chaplin went on: 'The bear get closer and closer, and everyone thinks he's going to make me his next meal. But just as it seems he's about to leap on me, he turns off the path and ambles back into the trees.'

I nodded again. 'Well – ?'

'Well,' said Chaplin, leaning forward to make his point, 'I defy you to name one comedian who wouldn't have played that scene by turning round,

seeing that bear, reacting – and running. By
not seeing the bear, it was that much funnier.' I
can't speak for the other comics in the world, but I
suspect he was right.

Charlie Chaplin had a dark side to him, which
may sound surprising when you think of the
laughter he brought to millions over so many
generations. Call it a mean streak, if you like. I saw
it for myself one day when his son Michael and my
own son Peter were arrested for – wait for it! –
wading into the fountains at Marble Arch and
taking out some of the coins that they found in the
water.

Marble Arch, of course, was once better known
as Tyburn. This wasn't an actual hanging offence,
but I was worried that the boys might get a police
record.

Chaplin was on a visit to London, staying in his
usual suite at the Savoy. I phoned ahead, and called
by to talk to him.

'I know it's a ridiculous charge,' I said. 'But just
suppose they get a magistrate with no sense of
humour? They could just get convicted.'

Chaplin's answer stunned me. 'You know my
son Michael,' he said flatly. 'He is not a very attractive boy.' In fact Michael had become something of
a hippy, growing his hair long and joining the
flower-power brigade.

But I was aghast. 'Charlie, what kind of answer
is that? Do you want your son to get a police
record?'

He looked at me with those cold eyes under the

white wispy hair. 'You do what you like. I don't want to have anything to do with it.' And he got up and walked out of the room.

His lovely wife Oona had been sitting nearby, listening. Now she said: 'Larry, get a good lawyer, and I'll split it with you.'

I got them a good lawyer – and we had a stroke of luck. The magistrate had a sense of humour, and I suspect the name Chaplin added bonus points to the defendants, too. I sat in court to give them moral support. The dialogue could have come from a *Carry On* film script.

Magistrate to prosecuting police officer: 'I fail to understand why this case has been brought before me.'

Policeman to magistrate: 'They took coins out of the fountain at Marble Arch, your honour.'

Magistrate to policeman: 'Well, why shouldn't they?'

Policeman to magistrate: 'The coins are the property of Westminster Council.'

Magistrate to policeman: 'Will you please inform me why the council chooses to keep its money in a fountain?'

Case dismissed.

I played tennis with many of the great and the good in Hollywood. John Garfield was a face I often saw over the net. He was only a year older than me, born in New York as Julius Garfinkle, a name he wisely changed when he took up acting.

The trouble with walking out on to a court opposite John was that you always had to let him win. We all had to. For why, you ask? Answer – because he would get very worked up if he was losing, and actually jump up and down on the court with rage. He had a heart condition, and we were worried stiff that he might have a coronary on court. In the end he did die of a heart attack in 1952, at the age of thirty-nine. As far as his friends were concerned, we all agreed: Christ, let him win!

Other famous names I've faced include Gilbert Roland, son of a Spanish bullfighter and as suave and immaculate on court as he was on screen; Paul Lukas, one of the great film villains; and Richard Conte, who made such an impact in the first *Godfather* movie but was a sucker for a passing shot on a tennis court.

When I tried to put him right, he said: 'Listen, Larry, I'm paying Tilden $50 an hour to coach me, and he says: "Serve and go to the net." Do you know more than Bill Tilden?'

I said: 'Dick, if I was your coach, I'd say: "Serve, and go to your room."' For some reason he didn't find that at all funny.

Burt Lancaster was another actor who took his game a little too seriously. One time he was on the next court at the Beverly Hills Club, playing against his coach Nick Ravat in front of a crowd of high-society glitterati. Burt was always hugely competitive, but this day he was in overdrive, arguing over every point.

'That ball was *in!*' Time and again I heard him

querying his coach's professional eye. 'That one was out! In . . . out!' It started to sound like a boat race.

Finally there was an almighty crash as Ravat flung his racquet on the ground, and stormed off the court. Over his shoulder, he shouted: 'Fuck you, and fuck tennis, too!' He left Burt open-mouthed, staring after him.

Next day they were back again, still arguing.

Recently I was back at the Beverly Hills Club, playing in a charity tournament on behalf of handicapped tennis players. A man appeared out of the crowd, came up to me, and asked: 'Mr Adler, would you mind if I introduced you to my wife?'

'Sure,' I said, and followed him over to the stand, where he pointed out a lady in the front row.

As I shook her hand, he said in a voice that carried across to the pavilion, and beyond: 'See, honey, I told you he wasn't dead!'

Lamely I responded: 'You haven't seen me play tennis.' But it was still game, set and match to him.

One year I heard from a tennis friend that Bjorn Borg was about to pull out of Wimbledon with a groin strain. I remembered something: back home I had a little machine that eases pain by means of a pair of electrodes powered by two batteries. You simply wet the electrodes and apply them to where it hurts.

My friend asked: 'Would you loan it to Bjorn?'

'Of course.' I dropped it round to the Holiday Inn at Swiss Cottage in north London where the

Swedish ace was staying. I heard no more – but Borg went on to win Wimbledon.

A year later I found myself at the same table following an exhibition match he had given in Battersea Park. I introduced myself. 'Mr Borg, my name is Larry Adler – '

'Ah,' he cried, before I could say any more. 'You're the man who saved Wimbledon for me.'

He was a gentle, sweet guy with perfect manners. But he's still got that machine.

John McEnroe is a jerk. That is my considered opinion, and I have found no reason to change it. I was talking with him once in a marquee at Wimbledon during a reception, and he revealed that his real ambition was to play the guitar, either solo or in a group.

I told him: 'Do you know that I have recorded with Django Reinhardt?'

McEnroe looked blank. 'Who's he?' he asked.

I walked away.

That same year I was watching him on Court One. There was the usual argument over a line decision. I turned to the man next to me, and said: 'You know, that guy could get into an argument with his own answering machine!'

'What makes you think he doesn't?' was the reply. I looked closer. Oh-oh! It was McEnroe's father. Well, he should know.

How do I rate John McEnroe? As a tennis player, a genius. As a human being, a schmuck!

At Wimbledon, which for me is the equivalent of an annual religious pilgrimage, I found a seat that

was marginally better than the Royal Box. In 1977 I
had been introduced to Jack Yardley, the legendary
head groundsman, at Queen's Club the week
before, and he invited me for the fortnight. No
ticket – but no need.

I met him at the gates, and he took me to watch
the Centenary Celebrations on the Centre Court,
with veterans like Lew Hoad, Don Budge, Jean
Borotra, Bobby Riggs, Jaroslav Drobny and Jack
Kramer lined up, Wimbledon champions all.

With the ceremony over, Jack told me to come
back at 1.45 p.m., fifteen minutes before play was
due to start. When I got there, I found he had placed
a canvas chair for me right on the edge of the turf,
like a film director about to call 'Action!' The players
practically had to clamber over me to get on court.

When I tried to thank him in the bar later, Jack
simply said: 'This is only the first day.'

I sat there for the entire tournament, a lone figure
in solitary splendour, challenged only by Virginia
Wade who knocked against my seat as she passed,
and hissed: 'My God, Larry. What are you doing
here? *Nobody* is supposed to be sitting here.'

'Tell you later,' I said. I didn't even know what I
was doing there, or how I had been accorded such
a privilege. But at the end of those two marvellous
weeks I finally cornered Jack Yardley in one of the
marquees:

'Why me, Jack? Is it my intelligence, my looks,
my wit? That I can understand, but there must be
something else – '

Finally he told me. 'I play the mouth organ too,'

he said. But, unlike me, he was a thwarted musician. Years ago he had even auditioned for the Harmonica Rascals, same as me, same age – fourteen. Only he had been accepted, while I hadn't.

Unfortunately his father had forbidden him to join their tour, and that brought Jack's potential career as a harmonica player to an abrupt end.

But it got me a seat in Wimbledon for years to come. And I never begrudged the possibility that Jack Yardley could have been a better mouth organ player than me!

A few months later I was playing at a nightclub in New York, and there at one of the tables was Virginia Wade with a party of friends. After the show, I joined the table, and she said: 'Larry, would you like to hit a few next weekend?'

Well, what a story to tell! The club was on Long Island, but when I got out there I found to my horror at least five hundred women sitting around the court, just waiting to see Virginia.

'God, Ginny,' I said, 'I'm not going out there in front of those broads!'

'Yes you are,' she said firmly – and Virginia can be *very* firm. 'This is the only court available. It's here, or nothing – and I need the practice.'

Well, I went out there like a lamb to the slaughter. But bless her, Virginia made me look good! I knew what she was doing. She could have humiliated me, but in front of all those ladies she made it look like a battle. I even got a game off her.

Yes, I like that lady a lot.

One actor who followed the tennis scene as fanatically as myself was Cary Grant. We were sitting together in the Players' Box on Centre Court one day, when he suddenly said: 'You know, Larry, you're the only artist I ever envied?'

I was taken aback. 'Why?'

'Because you can put your career in your pocket, take it with you to any country in the world, and you don't need to speak the language to earn your next meal.'

I'd never thought of it that way. But come to think of it, Cary was right.

12

Genevieve

*'You've got a first-class mind, Mr Adler.
What a pity you never had the benefit of a
public school education.'*

Bertrand Russell

Whoever in their right mind would have thought that a film about a classic car with a girl's name could become a classic movie in its own right? Certainly not the Rank Organization, who rode to fortune on her running-board. Or even the stars themselves, who had no idea they were at the wheel of the surprise hit of the year.

I'm talking about *Genevieve*, of course. Dare I say it – yes, indeed I dare! – it was vintage stuff. A breezy, happy-go-lucky story centred around a veteran car rally from London to Brighton with all the predictable pitfalls – if not pit stops – that beset the quartet on board. And what a cheery bunch they were: Kenneth More, John Gregson, Dinah Sheridan and the gorgeous Kay Kendall, the bubbly brunette who became known as the 'strumpet voluntary' after her spirited rendering on a bugle during one of the film's high spots.

Me, I wrote and played the catchy theme . . . and won an Oscar nomination for it, though my name never got on the programme on awards night.

Ah, *Genevieve*! That magnificent lady came thundering into my life on an otherwise unremarkable evening in 1953. I was idling away at the piano at a party in someone's house in Mayfair, making up the melody as I went along.

A lady named Vivienne Knight, who worked in public relations for J. Arthur Rank and would later become Mrs Patrick Campbell, came over. 'That's nice,' she said. 'What is it?'

People were always saying that to me. 'Oh, I'm just improvising,' I told her. Usual question, usual reply.

Next day the phone rang. On the line was Henry Cornelius, a producer who told me he was in the process of putting together a comedy about the annual London to Brighton car run. He had heard from Vivienne that I might be the man to write the score.

'Well – ' I was doubtful. Scoring for a film was a highly technical skill. Cornelius insisted that we meet, and suggested Les Ambassadeurs.

OK, there's no such thing as a free lunch – even for me. But Les A. was a tempting carrot. Who was I to resist an offer like that? Over the steak *au poivre* he put the proposition to me: could I handle it?

I said no, I couldn't.

'Vivienne says you can do it, and that's all I need to know,' growled Henry, in a tone that brooked no argument. 'At least take a look at the script.'

When I read the screenplay, I felt a sudden surge of excitement. You get those feelings sometimes, don't ask me why or how. But it happens. And when I saw the rough cut at a private screening-room at Pinewood Studios – I was hooked. Line and sinker!

The script was charming and witty. The characters likewise. The atmosphere was bubbling with light-hearted, essentially British fun where everything that could go wrong *did* go wrong, particularly when it came near the bedroom. It became one of the biggest British screen hits of all time.

More than that, anyone who saw it would for ever afterwards associate the name Genevieve with that film. And how often can you say that of a movie or a name?

Am I right, or am I right?

Oddly enough, one line in the script decided me. Early in the film, Dinah Sheridan is in the kitchen of her mews house. She calls up to her husband (John Gregson).

'Alan . . . proper lunch or proper dinner?'

That line decided me. It was so quaint. I *had* to do *Genevieve*.

It was a small-time movie, not expected to make any waves. The lead players were virtual unknowns, so you couldn't call them stars. Later would be another story. The entire film cost £100,000, which is probably marginally less than you pay the guy who massages Stallone or Schwarzenegger into life in today's overkill movie budgets.

My agent called me, and sounded gloomy. He had asked for £750. Cornelius pointed out that he didn't have £750. My price dropped to £500. Sorry, no. Henry couldn't raise that, either. Suddenly he didn't seem to have any money at all. Figuratively speaking, I was blowing in the wind.

'Forget it, Larry. This is a small-time outfit. Let it go, and we'll find another picture for you later in the year.'

He was right, of course. But one thing was nagging me. 'Nobody has ever asked me to compose before.' I thought of something else. 'Besides, I love the film and I want to do it.'

They offered me a percentage: two and a half per cent of the producer's share. It doesn't sound much, and it wasn't. But as the film took off I became richer than the actors, who each got a flat fee of £1,500 – yes, that's all – with no participation in the proceeds.

It's an old story, but it's still sad when it happens. John, Kenny, Kay and Dinah – if only they had been given a slice of the cake. When that movie opened to rave reviews ('One of the best things to have happened to British films over the past five years' – Gavin Lambert; 'Who he – Ed?') it was making a profit within the first month. As for me, I happily put my children through college on the proceeds.

But behind the scenes, trouble loomed. Not for the cast or crew, but for me. America was nervous. Meaning Hollywood and New York, where the power play was centred. What was the problem? In two words – Larry Adler.

The word got out that I was writing the score for *Genevieve*. Henry Cornelius was one of the good guys, an amiable soul celebrating his fortieth birthday as he ushered *Genevieve* safely through the winning tape on Brighton sea front on that June afternoon. As a would-be actor he had studied under Max Reinhardt, but he had really marked his card in the public perception as someone rather special with his 1949 comedy *Passport to Pimlico*, two years before *Genevieve* took to the road.

Henry called me into his office. He looked nervous and upset as he gestured me to a chair. It seemed that a call had come through from a top executive at the Rank Organization. The message was terse and to the point: get Larry Adler off the picture.

'They've been told that if your name is on the film, it won't get an American release,' he said, with a hopeless shrug.

The shadow of the blacklist had reached across the Atlantic. I looked at him. 'Corny,' I said. 'You're the one who put me on the film. If you want to take me off, just say so. I'll go. I don't want to do anything to hurt you, or the film. Do you want me off it?'

He shook his head. 'No. I love the stuff you've turned in. I don't want to lose it.'

'OK,' I said. 'Let my agent battle it out with Rank. I'll keep working on the score.'

Cornelius agreed. Later he would describe my methods as 'chaotic' – but they worked. I would get a sudden inspiration, and write the notes down on scraps of paper which I stuffed into my pockets, or pasted into a manuscript book. When I got to the studio I emptied my pockets on to a table, and went through the score with the musical director, Muir Mathieson.

Mathieson was the Scots-born veteran of literally hundreds of British film scores, either as composer or conductor, all the way back to the 1930s. His credits read like a musical roll of honour, from *The Scarlet Pimpernel* (1935) with Leslie Howard, Laurence Olivier's masterpiece *Henry V* (1944) and *Brief Encounter* (1945) with Trevor Howard and Celia Johnson to *The Seventh Veil* (1945) with James Mason and, later, *Lord Jim* (1965) which starred Peter O'Toole in the Joseph Conrad epic of Far Eastern skulduggery.

And here was Mr Mathieson, floundering through the notes of what Henry Cornelius dubbed my 'route map', and looking as lost as if he'd blundered into Hampton Court maze.

Corny told one interviewer: 'Even Larry didn't know how the pieces of paper followed each other. He works by memory, with some crazy method of his own. There was only one thing to do – we put our heads down for eight terrible hours trying to get the music into some sort of order, and finally got the route map together.

'It worked like this: you play the first four bars on page five, then the last twenty-three bars on page one. Repeat the four bars on page five, then play the little "bridge" which is on a separate piece of paper. You finish this sequence with ten bars, ringed in red ink, on page thirteen!'

The final score, in the words of critic Herbert
Kretzmer (who would later write the script of *Les
Misérables*), turned out to be 'one of the freshest and
most enchanting soundtracks ever heard on a
British film'.

I guess that exonerated me.

What it didn't do was spare me from the wrath
of the zealots in Hollywood who were still under the
McCarthy yoke, and thirsting for blood.

Behind the scenes, the in-fighting began. I had
no written contract, just a verbal agreement. That
was always good enough for me, as long as I knew
the parties involved. In this case, it left me with no
cards to play. I had to make a compromise if I
wanted to stay on the film – leave the billing to the
Rank Organization.

My agent was firm. Do it, Larry. You've really got
no choice. So, OK, I did it. But not without qualms.
I had never had this kind of pressure before, and I
didn't like it one little bit.

United Artists distributed *Genevieve* in the US.
She was booked for a New York opening run at the
Sutton Cinema on East 57th Street to see if she
would take off across the country.

Six weeks before opening date, the Rank Organization received the word that the US distributors
wanted my name taken off the print. Oh-oh!

They got it. *Genevieve* opened in New York to
excellent reviews, with the name Larry Adler
conspicuous by its absence from the credits.
Suddenly I was Public Leper Number One. I have
to say that few things have hurt me more than

having my name taken off the billing – though I got some satisfaction when most of the critics gave me credit for the music.

Out of the blue, that February, came a note from Ira Gershwin. 'Didn't you tell me that you had composed the score for *Genevieve*? The music has been nominated for an Oscar – but the composer is named as Muir Mathieson.'

And so it was. The ballad had been recorded by Percy Faith for Columbia, my own soundtrack was out on the same label, the music was published in Britain by 'Larry Adler Music'. No good. I was o-u-t – and I was one angry man. But what could I do?

Once the nominations were in to the Motion Picture Academy, they couldn't be changed. Rank had touched the forelock to the czars of Hollywood. I was the fall guy. On Oscar night my name was never even mentioned in despatches. But in the end it was that wonderful Russian composer Dimitri Tiomkin, of *High Noon* fame, who collected the treasured gold-plated gnome for *The High and the Mighty*.

Muir Mathieson was a gentle Scotsman, a peer among his own kind. I couldn't figure out how he had the effrontery to accept the Academy nomination for composing the score when both he and I knew it was my work, my blood, sweat and tears that had created it. Christ, we had been standing together on the sound stage at Shepperton as he conducted the orchestra!

Some weeks later, I met him at a charity function

and faced him with it, point blank. 'How could you?' I demanded, man to man.

'But Larry,' protested the grand old Scot. 'I just thought the Academy was giving me a special award for services to British film music.'

I believed him.

The odd thing about that film is that no one saw it coming. In Germany, it laid a large egg. Rank hated it – yes, *hated* it. Initially they put it on the shelf, and for a time it looked as if poor *Genevieve* wasn't going to take to the open road of a nation-wide release at all.

As for me, I had gone through all sorts of agonies after seeing the completed film in a private cinema in Soho, the first movie I had ever scored. Why, people were actually *talking* over my beautiful music, drowning it with dialogue and sound-effects! The lesson I learned was that the only time a film composer ever hears his score the way he wrote it is when it is being recorded on the sound stage.

While we were still in limbo, another picture opened for a six-week run at the Odeon, Leicester Square, the flagship cinema for the Rank Organization. It was a flop, and had to be taken off. The only film around was *Genevieve*.

The rest – well, you know it.

Despite all the flak that had come my way with the McCarthy witch-hunt, my friends stayed my friends – or most of them did, anyway. But private sympathy isn't the same as public support. Getting a foothold back on the ladder professionally in my own country – now *that* was a whole different mountain to climb.

Theatre owners were nervous of employing me. The fact that the movie distributors, United Artists, took my name off the *Genevieve* credits in the US – though not in the rest of the world – is proof enough that I was a hot potato to many in the executive suites of Hollywood and New York, where these decisions are made.

But slowly and surely I became *persona grata* again. McCarthyism was seen for what it was – a new, tainted word in our vocabulary. Eventually I would be back in the fast lane. But it took time.

My experience with *Genevieve* did nothing to put me off scoring for movies. In the end I would do three more. *The Great Chase* (1963) was a compendium of chase sequences from silent movies, with such legendary names as William S. Hart, Douglas Fairbanks (Senior) and Buster Keaton sprinting around the screen in double-quick time. How many living composers today can boast they scored for *those* three!

I found the most fun was providing the music for Keaton's train chase in *The General*. But then, I had always found Buster the funniest of all the early comics, including Chaplin.

In 1964 I was invited by Joseph Losey to score his film *King and Country*, a thought-provoking drama set in the trenches of World War I about a soldier (Tom Courtenay) court-martialled and shot for desertion. Dirk Bogarde played his defending counsel, and the strong cast included Leo McKern, Barry Foster and James Villiers. It was a sombre piece of work, and I created the music to match it.

A year later I scored *A High Wind in Jamaica*, an unlikely tale set in Victorian times about a group of English children on the way home from Jamaica being captured by pirates. The big guns were Anthony Quinn and James Coburn, but for me the film could never decide whether to be an adventure yarn or a serious drama.

But apart from *Genevieve*, the film music that meant most to me was the theme from *Touchez pas au Grisbi*, a 1953 French thriller about two crooks who steal a consignment of gold and live to regret it. A wonderful line-up of Continental talent included Jean Gabin, Jeanne Moreau and, in his first movie, the husky Italian actor Lino Ventura, whose thuggish looks made him a natural for gangster roles.

I was in Paris for a few days, and had lunch in Versailles with a publisher named Lou Levy, who was married to one of the Andrews Sisters. He told me he had the rights to the film. 'I think the title number would be just right for you,' he said. 'Come and have a listen to it.'

Next day I heard it in his offices, and I knew he was right. The tune was composed by Jean Wiener, and over the credits of the film it is played on a mouth organ by a French musician, Jean Wetzel. It is a first-class melody, haunting and beautifully constructed.

I made the record for Columbia, with a rhythm group behind my solo. Soon afterwards, an executive from the company called me up. 'There's a good chance you'll be nominated for the Grand Prix du Disque,' he said excitedly. This was the highest French award of its kind, and had never before gone to an American.

Sure enough, I won it. The awards were presented at the elegant Ritz Hotel, and I walked off with the trophy for the 'popular' classification. The *Herald-Tribune* devoted a big headline on page one to me – after all, I was the local boy making good.

The Grand Prix, and the advertising campaign that followed, must have boosted sales. *Grisbi* was top of the charts for eight weeks.

13

Love and Marriages

'A vasectomy means never having to say you're sorry.'

Larry Adler

I'll keep this short, as the bishop said to the actress. I've told you I'm a romantic, and it's true.

I was married twice. First to the lovely Eileen Walser, who modelled for the clothes designer Joseph Strassner. She was beautiful, witty, and – important, this – a good audience. We laughed a lot, which for me was equally important. Sex can be magnificent, but you don't spend all that much time making love. Most of the time you talk, if you're lucky. And I was very lucky.

The other day someone worked out that if you have sex twice a week for fifty years, you will probably have spent no more than four hundred hours entwined together in the sack. Whereas over that same period you will have probably both spent around twelve hundred hours brushing your teeth. Quite what that proves, I'm not sure, but I'm going to have a word with my dentist about it.

We tried to keep our wedding secret, because Eileen wanted it that way. She hated publicity. But the word leaked out, and the paparazzi swarmed around us at Marylebone Registry Office on the morning of 16 April 1938.

At least the honeymoon was a quiet one, disturbed only by the presence of a certain Hollywood actress who was also trying to remain out of sight of the media. Eileen and I had chosen a large but anonymous seaside hotel in Rottingdean, down the coast from Brighton. We checked in under phoney names, determined to keep it our secret.

But on our first night as we left the dining-room – a voice cried: 'Larry!' I knew that voice. Christ, the *world* knew that voice! A pair of heavy-lidded blue eyes fixed me with a beady gaze. 'What on *earth* are you doing here?'

'May I introduce you to my bride,' I said weakly. 'Eileen, meet Miss Bette Davis.'

The *grande dame* of Hollywood was in Britain, strictly incognito, to discuss a contract for a new movie. How we had chosen the same hotel, I'll never know. What I do know is that we played table tennis every day, and she whopped the hide off me.

Years later, in 1980, I was doing a show at the Tango Club in Chicago, and there she was in the audience. I couldn't resist it. 'Ladies and gentlemen,' I said. 'There is a lady sitting here tonight who a long time ago in England beat the hell out of me at table tennis – '

A throaty voice interrupted me from the floor. 'No I didn't. You trounced me every time.'

That's not the way I remember it.

That marriage produced my three children: first Carole, then four years later Peter, and five years after that, Wendy. Although our marriage broke down, ironically during the filming of *Genevieve* when both Eileen and I found ourselves involved elsewhere, I am proud to say that today my kids and I still have a warm and affectionate relationship.

My second wife was a journalist named Sally Cline. In 1965, by now divorced, I appeared at the Edinburgh Festival, where she came to interview me for *Queen* magazine. She gave birth to our daughter, Kate, whom I nicknamed 'Marmoset' – and the name stuck. Sadly, this marriage too broke down.

I'm one of the few men I know who doesn't mind a woman being brighter than me. I have no macho feeling at all. One lady who made a big impression on me was Maya Angelou, the world's best-read black woman writer. A friend of Martin Luther King, she has also been a self-confessed hooker, the madam of a brothel, a conductor on the San Francisco streetcars, a singer, dancer, poet and civil-rights worker. A fascinating lady, you will agree.

I met her in her dancing days. She was a chorus girl in *Porgy and Bess*, and I introduced myself to her when the cast threw a party in Milan. My God, that woman is bright! Maybe that's why we slept together that first night – I've always been attracted by a woman's mind, and if it leads to the bedroom, that's just fine.

We resumed our affair in Paris when I was play-ing at the Olympia Theatre and she came to town with *Porgy and Bess*. I had an apartment on the Left Bank, and we had a wonderful time, taking in the town for dinners after our shows and just being happy together.

The only bad moment in that period came the first night when we walked into a bistro together – and as we got through the door, I took her elbow, swung her round and walked her right out again. On the pavement she faced me angrily. 'What's the matter, Larry?' she demanded. 'Did you see somebody you knew? Are you ashamed to be seen out with a black girl?'

'Christ, Maya,' I said. 'Calm down! How can you say that to me?' I gestured through the window. 'You know I hate jukeboxes – and there's one blaring away in there. Take a look for yourself. I can't stand it.'

She took a look. 'Umm . . .' She didn't sound happy. It took me twenty minutes to convince her.

An extraordinary woman. 'If I'm happy, I smile,' she used to say. 'And even if I'm sad, I'll smile. And sometimes I'll sing.' And her poetry? 'It can tell us what human beings are. Poetry can tell us why we stumble and fall and how, miraculously, we can stand up again.'

She used to recite some of her poetry. I still remember lines from the 'Harlem Hopscotch':

All the people out of work,
Hold for three, then twist and jerk,
Cross the line, they count you out,
That's what hopping's all about.

Both feet flat, the game is done.
They think I lost . . . I think I won.

Yes, that's one lady I won't forget in a hurry. Not long ago Terry Wogan hosted a party for all the guests he had had on his show over the years. When I walked in – there was Maya. She threw her arms around me, and cried: 'Larry! I became an intellectual to please you!' Now *that's* what I call a compliment.

If I seem to fall in love too easily – well, I make no apologies. Like I say, I'm a romantic guy. It was when things were getting difficult with Sally that I met Lady Selina Hastings – and every love song I had played over so many years suddenly made sense. In short, I fell head over heels for that Lady.

At our first meeting, a dinner party given by a mutual friend, I realized Selina had never heard of me. The only famous Larry she knew was Larry the Lamb, of 'Children's Hour' fame. Not to bleat about the bush, I wooed her with the ardour of an old-fashioned suitor, wearing my heart unashamedly on my sleeve, and finally she succumbed.

Neither of us wanted children, so I performed the ultimate sacrifice – or, more accurately, had it performed on me. I recorded a radio programme called 'Quote, Unquote', and went straight from the BBC studio into the University College Hospital for a vasectomy. I had actually committed myself live on air by mentioning this on the programme to millions of doubtlessly enthralled listeners. Adding: 'A vasectomy means never having to say you're sorry!' Which at least got me into the pages of the *Penguin Book of Quotations* . . .

We never married, but we travelled the world together. But eventually we drifted apart, and I was alone again until a new love loomed on the horizon: the stylish Peruvian aristocrat I have already mentioned with the wonderful name of Tatiana von Saxe.

I shall resist puns about Saxe-appeal. Suffice it to say that at a party one night in Mayfair she came into my life, stayed there for eight years, and finally married someone else.

All I remember of our first date was the moment she looked deep into my eyes with that dark Peruvian gaze, and said: 'Larry, are you gay?'

I was taken aback, but responded with rapier-like wit: 'Not that I know of.'

But she persisted: 'Someone told me you are.'

'Well,' I said. 'Now you've given me a great incentive to prove otherwise.'

We took it from there.

Now? The woman in my life is Gloria Leighton, a lively lady with the unusual vocation of counselling people who have been wrongly convicted of shoplifting. You may have seen her on some of those TV discussion shows.

For myself, I'm alone, yes. But lonely – never! I've got my friends, my tennis, the telephone hot-line to London radio chat shows that I ring when the mood takes me – and usually get through – and I lead as hectic a social life as I want.

Besides, there's always my mouth organ for company.

14

Laughter and Music

*'You didn't tell that story very well, Bob.
Haven't you read my book on* How to Tell a
Jewish Joke?*'*

Larry Adler to Bob Monkhouse

'No, Larry. Haven't you read my book on
How to Shove a Harmonica Up Your Ass?*'*

Bob Monkhouse to Larry Adler

Apart from music, I am best known for my jokes,
my excruciating puns, my feud with *Private Eye*, my
phone calls to radio stations and letters to news-
papers, and my inability to turn down a free meal.

I plead guilty on all counts.

Laughter and music have been the staple diet that
has nourished me all my life. Without either, I
would have starved years ago.

As I said, I started out telling jokes mainly as
a self-defence mechanism to prevent myself as a
weedy little kid being bullied and beaten up by the
bigger boys. But there was another reason: when I
was growing up I was plagued by self-doubt over
my ability to carry on a decent conversation. I was
very aware of my inferiority at not having a
university education, and for years it haunted me.
But with jokes, I could be the hero of the hour.

You might find that hard to believe if you've heard me prattling away on the line to LBC or airing my views on a chat show. But it's true. That's the way it was, and it took me a long time to gain confidence – who said over-confidence? – that I now possess in abundance.

What kind of jokes do I like? Most kinds, as long as they're funny and told right. Surprising jokes. Silly jokes, but always with an inherent logic to them.

I was feeling a trifle mischievous one day in the office of *Harpers and Queen*, the glossy magazine for which I wrote a food column. We were discussing dumplings, and spotting Betty Kenward, the *grande dame* of the publishing house, passing nearby, I was able to pronounce 'four quenelles' loudly in her hearing, without any chance of retribution. You try it.

One story I really like was about the man who walked into a confessional, sat down in the booth, and said through the grille: 'Father, my name is Abe Cohen, I am eighty-seven years old, and last night I picked up a girl in a bar. I took her back to my flat, and we made love all night long, like I never made love before in my life.'

The priest said: 'Abe Cohen ... Abe Cohen ... Aren't you a Jew?'

'Yes, Father, I am.'

The priest was bewildered. 'Shouldn't you be talking to a rabbi? Why are you telling me?'

'I'm telling *everybody*!'

Another story that touches my particular

funnybone is the New Testament parable of the
woman taken for adultery. The villagers are about to
stone her to death.

Jesus comes forward and pronounces: 'Let him
who is without sin cast the first stone.'

The villagers hang their heads in shame, and put
down their stones. But one woman steps out of the
crowd with a brick, and whacks the girl over the
head with it.

And Jesus looks at her and says: 'Oh, Mother –
honestly!'

Now, isn't the logic of that quite impeccable?

Here's another one I like. A black man gets a job
at a huge corporation. On his first morning he asks
a senior executive, who happens to be white: 'Hey
man, where's the men's toilet at?'

The other looks at him and says haughtily:
'When you work for this company, you never, but
never, end a sentence with a preposition.'

The black man says: 'Of course, you're quite
right. Silly of me. May I revise the sentence.
Where's the men's toilet at – asshole?'

I can get away with jokes like that because I hate
prejudice of any kind, whether it's based on religion
or race, and everyone who knows me has got the
message by now. Like the other black man taking a
bus through New York, he asks the driver: 'Is this
49th?'

The driver replies: 'No, this is 50th. You're a block
past it.'

The guy says: 'What did you call me?'

I told you I like terrible puns.

Let me give you a practical example of an intellectual (me) in action. The other day I was driving through Camden Town in north London in my silver sports car, and swerved in front of a lorry. He had to jam on his brakes as I scooted off – but unhappily he caught up with me at the next set of lights.

He climbed down out of his cab, marched round to my window, and started to swear at me. I simply smiled, and when he paused for breath in his tirade, I said: 'I'll give you five pounds if you can say the next three sentences without using the word "fuck".'

He glowered at me. 'You're a wanker!' he said.

'That counts,' I told him, without losing my smile. And accelerated away as the lights turned green.

No money changed hands.

Or short and snappy. What is the sound a piano makes when you drop it down a mineshaft?

Answer: A flat minor.

My son Peter has inherited my off-beat sense of humour. When he was just a kid he drew a cartoon and sent it to me. It showed him in costume in the school play dressed as Hamlet, centre stage. He had obviously dried up. The prompter is hissing: '. . . or *not* to be!'

OK, it has been known for me to overstep the mark on rare occasions. I'm thinking now of that moment at the Savoy Hotel when Bob Monkhouse was holding forth at a Variety Club charity lunch. Bruce Forsyth, Ernie Wise, Jimmy Tarbuck and an assorted gaggle – or giggle – of comics were there in support of the Sunshine Homes. As usual, there was a VIP reception prior to the lunch in a private room off the main Lancaster Suite where the occasion was taking place.

Bob, who is a brilliant story-teller, was surrounded by a host of ardent listeners, sipping (or swilling) pre-lunch aperitifs, their ears metaphorically glued to every word as he launched into a Jewish joke. I hung around on the edge to pick up the punch-line, even though I knew the story. I can't remember it right now, because so many have flowed under the bridge.

What I do remember is that Bob told it badly. At least, I thought he did. I pride myself on my rendering of Jewish stories, on my immaculate timing, the accent, every little detail.

Bob got a laugh, of course. Which is when me and my big mouth piped up. 'You didn't tell that story very well, Bob. Haven't you read my book on *How to Tell a Jewish Joke*?'

Bob turned to me face on. Without so much as a pause he retorted: 'No, Larry. Haven't you read my book on *How to Shove a Harmonica Up Your Ass*?'

There have been occasions in my life when even I have been left lost for words. This was one of them. Bob slipped me a quiet 'That'll teach you, big mouth' wink, and went off to take his seat at the top table a few places from myself. Lesson: never tangle with a professional. Especially one who has ten thousand stories on file, as he has. Besides which, nobody tells a joke better than Bob Monkhouse.

Unless it's a Jewish joke, that is.

Right, Bob?

Another of Larry's favourites for you. Two fellows are mountain climbing. One suddenly loses his grip and plunges two thousand feet into the valley. His friend looks out over the precipice and yells: 'Seymour! Are you all right?'

'I'm fi-i-ne,' comes a weak voice back. 'I – I can't move my arms, or my legs. But otherwise I'm fine.'

'Seymour, I'm going to lower you a rope. Catch it in your teeth. I'll haul you up.'

He lets a rope down. Seymour grips it in his teeth, and the friend starts pulling. It takes nearly two hours of sweat and strain, but finally Seymour is near the top, teeth clenched on the rope.

The friend leans over as his buddy dangles beneath him. 'Ah, Seymour, thank God. It's good to see you, fella! How are you feeling?'

'I'm . . . fi-i-i-ne . . .'

The idea of poor Seymour hurtling off into the abyss again touches a cruel chord. Life can be a bitch sometimes.

Gossip columns and satirical magazines have put me through the wringer. But that's OK. I bear them no ill will. I know I'm a ham, see. But I don't do anybody any harm. I'm not a harmful ham.

My feud with the satirical magazine *Private Eye* went on for close to twenty years, and I love-hated every minute of it. Indeed, my hobbies in *Who's Who* include: 'Writing letters to *Private Eye*'.

It all began at one of the celebrated *Private Eye*

luncheons they used to hold periodically in Soho. I was one of the celebrity guests, and happened to mention how I had offered the *Sunday Times* critic Alan Brien thirty-five pounds if he could get a Richard Nixon joke into his column. He put it into his copy, but was overruled by his features editor, and it was taken out.

I told the joke at the table.

'At the height of the Watergate scandal Nixon's press adviser Ron Ziegler came up with a great idea. "We're going to get you circumcised. That'll get all the Jews behind you. You really need their vote, it'll work wonders for you, and make headlines."

'So they send for a *mohel*, the man who performs the operation. He goes into the bedroom with Nixon, and he's in there three hours. Finally he comes out, exhausted.

'"It's impossible," he says. "I can't do it. There's no end to this prick!"'

The writer and satirist Auberon Waugh was at the lunch. In the next issue of the *Eye* he ran the joke, then demanded thirty-five pounds off me. I refused. The offer was to Alan Brien to get the story into a national newspaper.

Waugh then launched a huge attack on me in his column in the *Eye*.

What should I do? Should I sue? No, that would be too pompous. Instead I wrote a funny letter, which they published.

Another attack, another letter. And so it began. I started to feel one of the family. They made a Christmas record, and the editor Richard Ingrams actually paid me a fee of £100 to play on it.

Eventually he would move on to edit a new magazine targeted at the elderly and called, somewhat adventurously in these youth-oriented times, *The Oldie*. Ian Hislop, another marvellously Machiavellian character, took over the hot sea at the *Eye*, and the feud faded. But it was fun while it lasted.

Epilogue

You've all heard of roast lamb. How about roast Larry the Lamb? To celebrate my eightieth birthday, my friends laid on a Roast. For the uninitiated, a Roast is where your so-called chums gather gleefully together over a banquet and tell the most insulting stories they can muster about their dearest pal.

Now an insult is defined as 'To speak or treat in a callous or contemptuous way . . . to reveal a disdainful estimate of someone . . .'

Well, on that February night at Le Buffet restaurant in Hendon, north London, disdain flowed as freely as the wine when 110 guests and half a dozen of my closest friends leaped to answer the call: Trash Larry.

The cognoscenti of erstwhile Fleet Street and the arts gathered at the top table to say their piece. The greying but still twinkly Richard Ingrams, former editor of *Private Eye*, and now my boss on *The Oldie*, where I write a monthly video column. The mischievous impish face of columnist Peter McKay that stares out at you from the pages of the *Sunday Times* and the London *Evening Standard*. TV presenter Michael Freedland, scriptwriter Alan Plater. The MC was David Jacobs.

And my old tennis sparring partner Victor Lownes, the rudest man I know (apart from myself), who had flown across the Atlantic for the joyous privilege of head-butting Larry, and getting a good meal into the bargain.

It was an epic night. Stand-up comic Joe Dingle set the tone by telling us how he had been driving his Vauxhall from Walsall to Southall, when he was stopped by a policeman who demanded to know what he'd got in his car. Vaux-hall, Wals-all, South-all, you could see it coming. Pause in anticipation. Then: 'Nothing,' said Joe.

I preferred his story of how he checked into a motel in the States at midnight to find just a Gideon bible and a note by his bedside: 'If you're an alcoholic, dial the following numbers.' He dialled it. It was an off licence. Nice one.

The Roasters lined up like gleeful schoolboys. McKay drew the audience along with the story of how I had met Tina Turner in a hotel, persuaded her to spend the night with me, and after an hour of passionate love-making had told her: 'I need to sleep. But only for two minutes. But in that time I want you to hold on to my organ – not my harmonica, the other one.' She did so. And after just two minutes, fully revitalized, we went at it again.

When it was over, same request. Hold on to my organ for two minutes ... And so it went on throughout the night. In the morning an exhausted Tina exclaimed: 'How on earth do you do it, Larry? What is it about holding your organ that gives you such energy?'

Me: 'It isn't that, Tina. The last time I slept with a woman, she pinched my wallet!'

It was left to Lownes to describe my 'left-wing looniness', and the causes I espouse 'which can best be described as "lost" – or they damn well should be!' Before revealing the story of my seventy-fifth birthday, where he arranged for a hooker to arrive at my apartment, announcing: 'I've got a song for you, a cake, and super sex.' She sang me a song, produced a cake, and then said: 'Do you want super sex now?' I said: 'I'll take the soup.'

But a Roast at least gives the victim the chance for the last laugh. I began: 'I've had a lovely evening – but this isn't one of them.' And after a few more salutory quips, I produced my mouth organ and filled that room with a piece of history: playing 'Rhapsody in Blue' to the accompaniment of a digital piano with George Gershwin's own backing, his invisible fingers making the keys move, and the pedals too. His feet, his fingers.

The ghost of Gershwin entered the room for a recital that sent the years tumbling and memories vibrating in my mind. Was it really sixty years ago that we played together for the first time, on that unforgettable night before I set sail in the *Aquitania* to a new continent, a new adventure?

As midnight struck, and I moved into my eighty-first year, it sent a shiver up my spine to hear George play with me again.

* * *

Sting rang me. 'Where on earth were you?' he demanded. His voice was almost accusatory.

'I thought you were going to play,' he said. 'That's why I called you.'

Oh-oh. Indeed, he had called up the previous day to invite me to the first of his concerts at the Royal Albert Hall that night. I had gladly accepted, not only because Sting was a friend but because I rated him one of the finest musicians around.

There had been two tickets on the door in my name, seats in a VIP box, and a great show that went on for almost three hours. Afterwards I went home.

'Don't you remember last time?' he said now. 'I want you to do it again, every concert. What do you say?'

I remembered last time. His last Albert Hall concert, a year previously. Out of the blue he had invited me to step up on stage to accompany him in 'Shape of My Heart', one of the numbers on his Grammy Award-winning album *Ten Summoner's Tales*. It had worked a treat. So now – what could I say but, happily, yes?

There is no introduction, that's the best bit. Sting is halfway through his sell-out concert. Peering through a gap in the screens behind the stage, I look out on a sea of faces raised in homage to their personal guru, the fresh, eager faces of a new generation.

Out there in the huge amphitheatre of the Albert Hall are 6,000 people, swaying and chanting, clapping and stamping, disciples who have paid up to £20 to sit at the feet of the high priest of popular rock.

A girl standing in the front row is waving a pink parasol. Others light matches and wave them slowly from side to side in time with the rhythm. The stage is bouncing with blue and white balloons. Searing spotlights from the domed ceiling cast Sting's body into silhouette as he moves around the stage, sometimes getting so close to the edge that the nearest fans reach out and touch him.

Above us, the sound baffles are suspended like enormous brown upturned mushrooms. The acoustics at the Albert Hall have always been a bone of contention, but tonight the waves of sound wash into every corner, every crevice, and nobody is complaining.

Out in the darkness flashlights explode like fire-crackers as another number comes to an end. Vinny Colaiuta gives a last, spasmodic drum roll, David Sancious runs his fingers down the keyboard, and Dominic Miller bends the final notes on his guitar. Sting holds his own guitar high, and waits for the hubbub to subside.

Then, slowly, he starts into the haunting first notes of the blues refrain 'Shape of My Heart'.

And it's my cue.

He deals the cards to find the answer,
The sacred geometry of chance,
The hidden law of a probable outcome
The numbers lead a dance . . .

The evocative words come alive with the music. I am wearing my black kaftan with a slim gold chain around the neck, as I thread my way past the keyboard to the second microphone facing out to the audience. Unannounced, unheralded, unexpected. Sting keeps playing, says nothing. Miraculously, he doesn't have to. A murmur spreads through the crowd, rising to a rumble of recognition – then sudden, spontaneous applause as I go straight into the backing.

> . . . And if I told you that I loved you,
> You'd maybe think there's something wrong,
> I'm not a man of too many faces,
> The mask I wear is one . . .

At the end, as the last haunting notes slide away into the shadows, Sting sweeps a hand in my direction: '*Mister* Larry Adler!' That's all, but it's enough. This night, and every night to follow, the audience rise out of their seats in a standing ovation.

As always, I am deeply moved. How can I not be? So many years . . . so many miles . . . so many memories . . . and I am still being recognized by a whole new generation. In the end, that first night, I have to make what we call a 'beg-off' speech, or they'll never let me off the stage.

'Listen,' I tell them, 'I'm a little old to have any more kids. But if I could adopt a son, I'd like it to be Sting.'

He stands besides me with a big grin, bends into the mike. And says: 'Thanks, Dad!'

Balloons burst at my feet as I bow for the final time, and turn and walk off with the cheers still filling that giant auditorium.

Nobody sees the tears in my eyes.

Because, my friends, *that's* the way I want to be remembered.

George Gershwin: Biography

George Gershwin, the master composer of experimental jazz and a legend in his own musical lifetime, was born Jacob Gershvin on 26 September 1898, in Brooklyn, New York.

The noted composer of concert and popular music became one of the leading creative forces on the American musical scene, the only man to make the cross-over from jazz into the classical field. Along with his brother Ira, two years his senior, who wrote the lyrics, his timeless melodies spanned generations and brought joy to millions.

The contribution of the Gershwin brothers to American music is almost unequalled. Jazz combos never tire of improvising on their original tunes, nor do popular singers, serious recitalists, symphony orchestras, dance bands, and ballet and opera companies.

George's first show was the music for *Half Past Eight* in 1918. It lasted a week in Syracuse. But he bounced back in 1919 with 'Swanee', and when Al Jolson sang it in his show *Sinbad* the following year, George was on his way.

In the 1920s the Gershwin brothers worked together and separately to create an incredible list of all-time hits: 'Lady Be Good', 'Funny Face', 'Girl

Crazy', 'The Man I Love', 'Someone to Watch Over Me', 'Fascinating Rhythm', 's'Wonderful', 'I Got Rhythm' . . . to name but a few. The year 1924 saw the first performance of 'Rhapsody in Blue', with George himself at the piano.

During a visit to Paris in 1928 George conceived much of the ideas and music for *An American in Paris*, which has taken its place in the regular repertoire of symphony orchestras all over the world.

Described as 'an East Side boy who played ragtime by day and pored over Debussy by night', George in private life was a loner and noted romancer of beautiful women, among them actress Paulette Goddard. He was immortalized in celluloid in the 1945 film biography *Rhapsody in Blue*, which starred Robert (father of Alan) Alda.

In 1937 George was with Ira in Hollywood when he developed the severe headaches that later proved to be caused by a brain tumour. He died that same year during an operation to remove the tumour – at the tragically young age of thirty-eight.

The noted broadcaster and jazz authority Alistair Cooke summed up the man and his music in the following tribute: 'Of all the gifted men who made the twenties and thirties a golden age of song, George Gershwin was the truest original.'

JONATHAN SHALIT PRESENTS

THE GLORY OF GERSHWIN

Featuring
LARRY ADLER
Produced by
GEORGE MARTIN

OLETA ADAMS - *Embraceable You*

LARRY ADLER & GEORGE MARTIN - *Rhapsody in Blue*

CHRIS DE BURGH - *Do What You Do*

KATE BUSH - *The Man I Love*

CHER - *It Ain't Necessarily So*

SINEAD O' CONNOR - *My Man's Gone Now*

ELVIS COSTELLO - *But Not For Me*

PETER GABRIEL - *Summertime*

ELTON JOHN - *Someone to Watch Over Me & Love Is Here To Stay*

JON BON JOVI - *How Long Has This Been Going On*

MEAT LOAF - *Somebody Loves Me*

ROBERT PALMER - *I Got Rhythm*

COURTNEY PINE - *Summertime*

CARLY SIMON - *I've Got a Crush On You*

LISA STANSFIELD - *They Can't Take That Away From Me*

STING - *Nice Work If You Can Get It*

WILLARD WHITE - *Bidin' My Time*

& Introducing

ISSY VAN RANDWYCK - *I'll Build A Stairway To Paradise*